A

SAINSBURY COO OK

T

CH S

GLYNN CHRISTIAN

CONTENTS

Published exclusively for J Sainsbury plc
Stamford House Stamford Street
London SE1 9LL
by Martin Books
Simon & Schuster Consumer Group
Grafton House 64 Maids Causeway
Cambridge CB5 8DD

ISBN 0 85941 801 4

First published September 1992
Second impression September 1993

Printed in Italy by Printer Trento

THE AUTHOR

Glynn Christian is best known as an entertaining and innovative television chef. He appeared on BBC-TV's Breakfast Time for four years and is a regular guest on other shows.

Born in New Zealand, where he worked as a radio and television writer, Glynn came to the UK in 1965. He developed his wide knowledge of ingredients and cooking while working as a travel writer throughout Europe and then through operating a delicatessen on London's famed Portobello Road.

A direct descendant of Fletcher Christian who led the mutiny on the Bounty, Glynn spent three years researching and writing Fragile Paradise, the only biography of his ancestor. Major food books include *The Delicatessen Handbook*, *The World Guide to Cheese*, *The Gourmet's Freezer* and for Sainsbury's *The Cooking of the British Isles* and *Pies, Pâtés and Terrines*.

Glynn's views on ingredients and how best to use them can be read every week in the Sunday Telegraph and the Sunday Mercury.

Pictured on the front cover: Traditional Roast Turkey (page 19) with accompaniments and Hackleback Potatoes (page 39).

Pictured on the back cover: see caption to pages 4/5.

The Traditional British Christmas Dinner: Smoked Salmon Ice Cream (page 12); Traditional Roast Turkey with Giblet Gravy (page 19), Bread Sauce (page 43), Cranberry Sauce (page 51) and Roast Potatoes, Celeriac Mash, Bacon Rolls and Chipolatas (all page 36); A Traditional Plum Pudding (page 72) and Rich Custard Sauce (page 79).

INTRODUCTION

Tradition is hard to define sometimes, but easy to recognise when it comes to Christmas. The great wealth of our Christmas customs is due in part to their antiquity: some are pre-Christian or even medieval in origin, while some were introduced only in the nineteenth century, popularised by Queen Victoria but very much as a consequence of the influence of Albert, her German husband.

Christmas puddings certainly have their roots in the most ancient of British cookery, a sort of fruity porridge, but became associated with celebration largely through the special affections of George I, our Hanoverian Georgie Porgy, Pudding and Pie king. Prince Albert revived interest in the plum pudding at Christmas feasts, and introduced decorated Christmas trees, contributing to a major change of British Christmas custom at a time when the popularity of Charles Dickens and the new habit of sending Christmas cards could spread such customs around the world. Fashion became tradition within decades.

If you go back further in time, beef and goose were once more popular than turkey; there was even a time when celebrating Christmas was banned by Cromwell and his Puritans, so tradition had to be reinvented after the restoration of Charles II.

Yet there is one superseding tradition of Christmas, to me the most important one: the comforting tradition of a large or small gathering enjoying a meal together, secure in the warmth of old friendships and bonds, welcoming new family members or guests and looking forward to another year.

In essence, we are celebrating an event which happened in the Eastern Mediterranean, and a time that gave us more than Christianity. Ancient feuds and fights over Jerusalem and the Holy Land led to the Crusades, holy Wars fought by knights, gentlemen and soldiers from all over Europe. Sometimes they won, often they did not.

But what they brought back from the Crusades conquered and ruled our kitchens for centuries. For the Crusaders brought back with them our first taste of black pepper, of ginger and cinnamon, mint and dried fruit, prunes and currants, and oranges too. Most of all they bought to our kitchens the voluptuous pleasures of rose-water and orange-flower water, both distilled directly from perfumed blooms and used in savoury and sweet dishes. Rose-water was probably as popular in Britain as vanilla and chocolate flavourings today, right up to the turn of the last century.

For the rich and powerful, food was never the same again, and the traditions of Eastern Mediterranean Arabic cookery became those of Britain for centuries. Mousses were made of beaten chicken flesh and ground almonds – and called blancmange. Meats were mixed with dried fruits, spices and sugars and baked in coffins (pastry shells) to become eventually our meatless Christmas meat pies. Food was coloured red with sandalwood or green parsley juice, or gilded with saffron or real gold leaf. The spices of the East became more associated with British cooking than our native herbs.

This book looks to those old ingredients for inspiration, but also celebrates the greater variety of produce available now. Today we can add elegance and refinement to ancient White Soup based on almonds, by including a wine from any continent of the world, and using celeriac rather than the coarser celery.

We can also call on the traditions and ingredients of the New World, celebrating both the origin of the turkey and also the vibrant colours and flavours of American vegetables; tomatoes and corn, peppers, beans and pumpkin, displayed mouthwatering in the picture on pages 16/7. Be rigidly British with a Golden Goose with Sage and Onion Stuffing (page 27) or ring the changes by serving a standing rib of beef tunnelled with sherry-flavoured pickled walnuts and wild mushrooms (page 24). If you don't have enough hands to help carve and serve, be really bold and serve Turkey Breasts in a Glazed Chestnut Overcoat (page 60), with all the hard work done the day before; you slice the stunning result as easily as a loaf of bread.

For me, whichever way we look for our Christmas culinary pleasure, the touchstone will always be the old flavours and ingredients of the Eastern Mediterranean, the traditions of the Crusaders. For nothing makes a house more welcoming than the scent of cooking spices, and a few ingredients add so much to the pleasure of hospitality for so little cost or effort.

I hope this book adds a little extra enjoyment to your favourite Christmas traditions and helps you discover new ones. Most of all I wanted to make Christmas entertaining fun for the cook. That's my most important tradition – if something seems too much trouble or keeps you away from the party too long, don't do it. Food is important at Christmas, but never so important as friends and family.

COUNTDOWN TO CHRISTMAS DINNER

★

CHRISTMAS EVE

Ensure a frozen turkey is defrosted. Make up stuffings. If the turkey is fresh or completely defrosted, prepare and stuff it now. Keep it cool. Calculate the bird's weight and then the cooking time; add one hour to allow the bird to come to room temperature before cooking and 30 minutes resting time after cooking. Subtract this total from the time you plan to eat to establish the time to start cooking.

★

Calculate steaming time of pudding.

★

Make up any sauces, relishes, etc. which are suitable to reheat in the microwave or over a pan of hot water. Prepare bacon rolls. Prepare your first course ingredients.

★

Check you have enough pots, pans, bowls, etc. for your menu and plan hob or oven space. Now is the time to change the menu!

★

Choose the plates, cutlery, crystal; set table if practical, leaving glasses upside down.

★

Make everyone in the house agree to breakfast at the same time so you (a) get a clear kitchen (b) know when you can get some help.

CHRISTMAS MORNING

Preheat the oven. Stuff the turkey if not done. Start the turkey.
Set the timer to remind you when to start the pudding.

★

Get help to prepare the vegetables and set the table if not done.

★

Firmly choose who will be in charge of ice, drinks, and music.

90 MINUTES BEFORE SERVING:
Begin roasting vegetables. If you forget, boil them and then paint them with oil and brown under the grill.

★

60 MINUTES BEFORE
start bacon rolls, chipolatas, etc.

★

30 MINUTES BEFORE
put water into saucepans for vegetables and begin gently reheating sauces if you have no last minute microwave plans.

★

Remove turkey and put on to warm plate; allow fat to rise in roasting tin, pour off and then make gravy.

★

Turn up heat in oven to complete vegetable roasting.

★

Complete preparing first course.

★

15 MINUTES BEFORE
ensure all cooking water is very hot, keep covered. Put main course plates in oven. Serve first course.

★

DURING CLEARING
cook remaining vegetables except brussels sprouts. Garnish turkey. Bring in hot plates and roasted vegetables. Get someone to start carving.

★

DURING CARVING
bring in hot sauces, cook the sprouts and other delicate green vegetables, then serve immediately.

★

FIRST COURSES

CREAM OF ALMOND AND CELERIAC SOUP WITH WHITE GRAPES

Preparation time: 25 minutes + 20 minutes cooking Serves 6

500 g (1 lb) celeriac, chopped roughly

50 g (2 oz) butter

300 ml (½ pint) Gewurztraminer or medium-dry white wine

125 g (4 oz) ground almonds

600 ml (1 pint) chicken, veal or vegetable stock

600 ml (1 pint) milk

white pepper

24 white grapes

'White Soup' was one of Britain's oldest special soups for entertaining, made from ground almonds and flavoured with celery. It went out of fashion once fewer people had a stock pot on the boil and everyone had less time to grind their own almonds.

Now it can be made in a trice, but this is a lighter modern version using ground almonds, celeriac and the fresh stock you buy in cartons. By varying the basic stock you can appeal to individual preferences, or make a vegetarian version.

Gently fry the celeriac in the butter in a covered saucepan until most of the butter has been absorbed. Add the wine and simmer uncovered until the wine has boiled away. Add the almonds, stock and milk and simmer for about 20 minutes or until the celeriac is really tender. Liquidise in a blender or food processor and strain through a sieve, using the back of a soup ladle to force as much through the sieve as possible. Add a little white pepper to taste.

Seedless grapes may simply be halved and popped on to the soup when it's served. Otherwise they should be de-seeded and it will be much more impressive if you have also peeled them. Do this by pouring on boiling water, leaving for 5 minutes, then removing the skins with a knife. Halve them or not according to your whim.

This soup may also be served chilled, when you will probably prefer to thin it with extra stock, wine or cream. Either way, serve the soup with the remainder of the bottle of Gewurztraminer.

Pictured on page 21

ROASTED RED PEPPER MOUSSELINES WITH WATERCRESS SAUCE

Preparation time: 40 minutes + 30 minutes cooking Serves 6

750 g (1½ lb) red peppers

4 garlic cloves, unpeeled

2 teaspoons olive oil

4 eggs, beaten

250 g (8 oz) curd cheese

about 1 tablespoon lemon juice

about 1 teaspoon garlic vinegar

paprika

6 sprigs of watercress

For the sauce:

2 large bunches of watercress

142 ml (¼ pint) carton of double cream

75 g (3 oz) unsalted butter

A brilliantly coloured combination of direct flavours, served just warm, so no need to rush; a bright, interesting vegetable accompaniment to main courses too, without the sauce.

Preheat the oven to Gas Mark 3/160°C/325°F, and preheat the grill on a low setting. Slice the red peppers from top to bottom to make the biggest flat pieces you can. Remove the seeds and fleshy ribs. Lay them skin side up on a baking sheet under the grill and grill until soft and cooked through, 10-15 minutes. Turn up the heat to medium and watch carefully until all the skins are charred and blistering, about 5 minutes. Remove the pepper pieces from the grill and cover with a tea towel until cold. Peel away the skins.

Poach the garlic cloves in a little water in a small saucepan for about 15 minutes or until really soft. Peel off the skins. Purée with the peppers and oil. Force through a sieve if necessary to get a really smooth purée. Beat the eggs into the cheese gradually, followed by the pepper and garlic purée. Sharpen gradually with lemon juice and garlic vinegar a little at a time; don't overwhelm the pepper flavour.

Lightly oil 6 ramekins or dariole moulds and sprinkle with paprika. Put a sprig of watercress at the bottom of each. Divide the mixture evenly between the ramekins and stand them in a roasting tin of boiling water. Cover the tin with a dome of foil and cook for about 30 minutes. The mousselines are done when a knife put into the middle comes out cleanly. Let them sit in the ramekins for 10 minutes before serving.

To make the sauce, pull off all the best watercress leaves from the stems. Chop the stems and remaining leaves roughly and toss them in a small hot pan for about 5 minutes until almost all the liquid created has evaporated. Add the cream and simmer for 8-10 minutes. Strain the cream through a sieve into a clean bowl, pressing the stalks hard to get every last drop. Put the bowl over a pan of hot water. Whisk 50 g (2 oz) of the butter bit by bit into the sauce and keep it warm over the hot water.

When ready to serve, toss the reserved watercress leaves in the remaining butter until they are wilting; then divide them between the plates, arranged in small circles. Run a knife around the inside of each ramekin and tip each mousseline on to the watercress leaves. Surround with the warm sauce.

SMOKED SALMON ICE CREAM

Preparation time: 15 minutes + freezing — Serves 6–8

250 g (8 oz) smoked salmon, chopped finely

175 g (6 oz) ricotta cheese, sieved

1 tablespoon vodka

fresh lime juice to taste

a dash of Tabasco sauce

142 ml (1/4 pint) carton of double cream

A delightfully different way to serve smoked salmon.

Process the salmon in a food processor or blender with the ricotta cheese until really smooth. Add a little vodka to help if necessary. Turn it into a bowl and flavour with lime juice, making it slightly sharper than you like to compensate for the sweetness of the cream. Add a dash of Tabasco. Whip the cream until it is rather like a thick custard, holding its shape but not peaky. Fold it evenly into the salmon mixture and then transfer the mixture to a freezerproof container and freeze. Remove it from the freezer half an hour before required and serve in one of the following ways:

- Scoop the ice cream on to a small square of smoked salmon, add a few cooked prawns and some salad leaves; grate lime zest directly over the top.
- Arrange scoops of ice cream in artichoke bottoms, lightly dressed with hazelnut oil and lemon or lime juice; sit the artichokes on a small salad of mixed leaves.
- Substitute small scoops of ice cream for the quail eggs in Smoked Salmon Nests with Quail Eggs (page 13).

- Layer with prepared seafood and a spicy mayonnaise in a tall glass to make the ultimate seafood cocktail.
- Finely slice or fan an avocado half per person and put the halves on to plates, pit sides up; scoop the ice cream into the avocados and grate lime zest over them.

Pictured on pages 4/5

SMOKED SALMON NESTS WITH QUAIL EGGS

Preparation time: 20 minutes — Serves 6

12 quail eggs

3 tablespoons groundnut or corn oil

2 tablespoons walnut oil

1–2 tablespoons sherry vinegar

75 g (3 oz) mixed salad leaves

250 g (8 oz) sliced smoked salmon

pepper

grated zest of 1/2 a lemon or lime, to garnish

A pretty way to serve smoked salmon. Choose salad leaves with contrasting colour and texture – lambs lettuce, radicchio, escarole, frisée.

Put the quail eggs into cold water and bring to the boil; simmer for 1 minute. Cool them completely under cold running water, cracking the shells lightly. Shell the eggs, rinse and reserve them.

Whisk together the oils and vinegar; season with a little pepper. Toss the salad leaves in the dressing, then transfer them to a sieve and allow them to drain over a bowl for a few minutes. Reserve the drained dressing.

If you are not using pre-sliced salmon, cut it into strips 4 cm (1 1/2 inches) wide. Just before serving, divide the salmon into 6. Slightly twist each piece as you make a circle on each plate. Adjust so that the twisted salmon stands high rather than lies flat. Fill each circle with salad and add 2 quail eggs to each. Scatter any extra salad leaves around the plates. Drizzle a little of the extra dressing over the quail eggs. Grate a little lemon or lime zest over each plate to serve.

Pictured on pages 76/7

POACHED VEGETABLES IN A BALSAMIC VINEGAR MARINADE

Serves 6

Preparation time: 25-30 minutes + 4 hours marinating + 2 hours chilling

600 ml (1 pint) vegetable stock

300 ml (1/2 pint) medium-dry white Italian wine

2 tablespoons olive oil

1-2 tablespoons balsamic vinegar, or to taste

150 g (5 oz) mange tout, topped and tailed

125 g (4 oz) baby sweetcorn cobs

125 g (4 oz) courgettes, sliced diagonally into 1 cm (1/2-inch) lengths

375 g (12 oz) mixed red and yellow peppers, de-seeded and cut into 3 cm (1 1/4-inch) cubes

250 g (8 oz) carrots, cut into 3 cm (1 1/4-inch) slices

3 tablespoons coarsely chopped parsley, to garnish

A stimulating low-calorie first course, or a light luncheon with plenty of bread. Balsamic vinegar from Italy has an amazingly complex sweet-sour flavour and thus should be used with great restraint. Chicken, veal or fish stock may replace the vegetable stock if you prefer. Choose a favourite vegetable or make a mixture of complementary colours and textures: as well as the examples used below, you could try small fennel bulbs cut in half; neat barrels of leek; celeriac cut into thick batons; thick cucumber sticks; or green beans. Cook more vegetables in any leftover marinade or add it to a soup.

Mix the stock, wine and olive oil and simmer gently for 10 minutes; keep warm. Just before pouring the marinade over the vegetables, flavour it with balsamic vinegar; the amount will vary according to type but it should dominate at this stage for it will be diluted as it is absorbed by the vegetables.

Each vegetable should be lightly poached in boiling water, keeping its bright colour and a little crispness: 2-6 minutes should suffice. As they are done, arrange them in a large flat-bottomed dish. Pour the warm marinade over them and leave at room temperature for at least 4 hours. Then chill for about 2 hours, but do not serve directly from the refrigerator or much of the flavour will be hidden; just below room temperature is probably best. Baste the vegetables with just a little of the marinade and sprinkle them with parsley. Extra balsamic vinegar may be passed around.

GIANT PRAWNS AND CUCUMBER ON A TRUFFLED SAFFRON ASPIC BED

Preparation time: 30 minutes + about 4 hours chilling Serves 6

1/2 large cucumber, peeled

24 g (1 oz) packet of aspic powder

500 ml (18 fl oz) boiling water

1/2 teaspoon saffron strands

150 ml (1/4 pint) medium white wine

50 g (2 oz) bottle of summer truffle

500 g (1 lb) extra-large prawns, thawed if frozen

75 g (3 oz) mixed frisée, lambs lettuce, radicchio

For the hazelnut dressing:

2 tablespoons hazelnut oil

1 tablespoon vegetable oil

1 tablespoon white wine vinegar

Wide shallow soup plates and a cool storage place are essential for this; you probably won't have room in the refrigerator on Christmas Day. Elegant, refreshing and beautiful to see; the aspic is diluted with wine, so it becomes a wobbly savoury jelly that melts in the mouth. The truffle is optional. The aspic may be further decorated, say with sprigs of fresh dill, flat-leaf parsley or fresh coriander leaves.

Cut the cucumber in half lengthways and scoop out the seeds. Slice across to make half moon shapes about 1 cm (1/2 inch) wide. Poach them in boiling water for 5 minutes; then cool them under running water in a sieve. Arrange them in the bottom of 6 shallow, flat-bottomed soup plates. Dissolve the aspic powder in the boiling water, and stir in the saffron and the wine.

When cool, ladle the aspic carefully into the soup plates. Slice the truffle very thinly and divide the pieces evenly amongst the plates. Divide half the prawns amongst the plates too.

Pull the frisée and radicchio into small pieces but leave the lambs lettuce in clumps. Make a high mound in the centre of each plate with about two-thirds of the salad leaves. Arrange the remaining prawns on the salad, with some of them dipping into the aspic. Let the aspic set before moving the plates to a really cold place to chill thoroughly – for up to 4 hours. Make up the dressing and toss the rest of the salad in this. Pile it on top of the salad already in place. Serve at once.

An American-style Christmas Dinner: Roast Turkey with Blueberry Wild Rice Stuffing (page 47); Cranberry Relish (page 52); Sweet Potato with Pecans (page 38); Succotash (page 38); Green Beans with Ginger (page 38); Tomato-Chilli Baked Pumpkin (page 38); and Gratin of Tarragon Courgettes (page 39); Pilgrims' Pudding with Butter Sauce (page 74).

CHILLED MELON AND LOBSTER SOUP

Preparation time: 15 minutes + overnight chilling Serves 6

2 ripe Galia melons

540 g (17 oz) jar of lobster bisque

2 tablespoons dry sherry or cognac

2 tablespoons greek-style yogurt

1 tablespoon chopped fresh mint

Made in minutes, a refreshing start to heavy meals. If some guests do not like alcohol, this addition can be made individually just before serving.

Scoop out the flesh of the melons and liquidise it. Strain through a fine sieve, then chill overnight, in a very tightly sealed container.

If the lobster bisque contains any pieces of lobster flesh these should be strained out. Stir in the dry sherry or cognac, cover and chill overnight.

Ladle the melon into shallow soup plates. Carefully pour the lobster bisque into the middle of each plate to make a filled circle. Use a knife to draw threads of the bisque into the melon, making a sunburst pattern. Mix the yogurt with the mint and put a blob into the middle of each plate.

WARM PEACH AND GAMMON SALAD, MINTED RASPBERRY VINAIGRETTE

Preparation time: 20 minutes Serves 4–6

1–2 garlic cloves, chopped

1 tablespoon olive oil

750 g (1 1/2 lb) gammon, cut into strips

1 radicchio

150 g (5 oz) mixed salad leaves

3 ripe but firm peaches, sliced

1 tablespoon hazelnut oil

6 tablespoons raspberry vinegar

2 tablespoons fresh mint leaves, torn roughly

This is a basic recipe to which you may make many changes. Any cooked meat is suitable, especially chicken, turkey or goose. Pears or apples may be used instead of peaches.

Fry the garlic gently in the oil without browning and then add the gammon. Cook until lightly browned, for about 8 minutes; meanwhile arrange all the salad leaves on a serving platter or individual plates. Push the gammon to one side, add the peaches and heat them through. Mix and tip on to the salad. Add the hazelnut oil, raspberry vinegar and mint leaves to the pan and swirl them over the heat for 1 minute. Pour the dressing evenly over the salad and serve.

MAIN COURSES

TRADITIONAL ROAST TURKEY WITH GIBLET GRAVY

Preparation and cooking time: see recipe

1 turkey

stuffing of your choice

1 onion, sliced

1 apple, orange or lemon, sliced

butter or oil for basting

For the giblet gravy:

giblets of the turkey

75 g (3 oz) butter

250 g (8 oz) onion, sliced finely

2 bay leaves

2 × 5 cm (2-inch) strips of orange zest

1/2 large celery stick, chopped

12 black peppercorns

600 ml (1 pint) red wine

300 ml (1/2 pint) fresh chicken stock

1 heaped tablespoon plain flour

salt

These days, the so-called traditional stuffings and accompaniments to the Christmas turkey are being seen as the main culprits that contribute to a feeling of over-eating. If you had not been told they were traditional would you really choose chipolatas and bacon, two types of potato, a starchy bread sauce and a bread-based stuffing? Of course not. Individually they are delicious, but all together they combine to make a mountain of starch and fat on the plate and there are many better ways to enjoy turkey. Still, what is perceived as tradition is difficult to change. Until you make some changes it is worth being certain that you are getting the best possible results.

There are very many misconceptions about roasting turkeys and other large birds. Trussing and basting, for instance, are leftovers from the time when all birds were cooked on a revolving spit. If you are cooking in an oven, trussing stops the heat getting to the thickest part of the legs and thus risks the breast being overcooked before the legs are done. Every time you open the oven to baste you drop the temperature dramatically and muck-up your cooking time calculations; anyway, basting does nothing at all to keep the flesh moist as the fats and juices cannot penetrate the skin. Bread stuffings are not traditional inside a bird. Bread sauce was only invented last century when pasteurisation made milk safe for the first time. A turkey should never be roasted on its back and using foil steams rather than roasts your bird!

Here's a checklist of what you should and should not do in preparing your bird, all guaranteed to give you a moist bird full of flavour, even if you have never cooked one before.

- Ensure the bird is fully thawed if it was frozen.
- Remove all trussing.
- Ensure all giblets are removed from inside.
- Cut out the wishbone (page 28), to make carving immensely more simple.

- Stuff between skin and breast and in the neck only, not in the body cavity.
- Put only sliced onion, apple, orange or lemon into the body cavity, which will produce steam and juices.
- Do not use bacon on the breast if you are serving bacon rolls.
- Do not waste butter or time on basting if you have stuffed the turkey between the skin and the breast; a generous oiling or buttering of the bird's skin is enough to make it turn brown.
- Make sure the prepared bird is at room temperature when put into the oven.
- Write down the combined weight of the bird and stuffings before it goes in the oven, so you don't forget the cooking time.
- As well as the cooking time, allow an extra 30 minutes for the bird to rest before you carve it – essential to ensure evenly moist and tender flesh.
- Most important of all, have no other food around when preparing the turkey; once you have finished, thoroughly wash and rinse all surfaces and implements used with very hot water containing a little household bleach.
- Size of turkey, quantity of stuffing and cooking times will all obviously depend on how many people you want to feed, and these have therefore not been specified in the recipe that follows.

To make the giblet gravy: start the day before for the best flavour. This is a richly flavoured gravy; if preferred, you can use only stock or just water, rather than the wine and stock.

Brown the giblets slowly but very well in half the butter for about 10 minutes. Remove them from the pan and melt the remaining butter. Add the onion and cook for 20–30 minutes until very soft and lightly browned. Return the giblets to the pan and add the rest of the ingredients except the flour. Bring to the boil, scraping up the browned crust from the bottom and then reduce to the barest simmer for 1½ hours, during which time the volume should halve.

Remove from the heat, cool, turn the gravy

A Georgian-style Christmas Supper: Cream of Celeriac and Almond Soup (page 10); Georgian Turkey Fricassee (page 23) with Cucumber and Artichokes (page 37); Cumberland Rum Nicky (page 79).

into a large bowl, cover it and chill overnight.

Remove the giblets and the fat from the top of the gravy. Strain the stock. When the turkey is cooked, pour off most of the fat and scrape and stir the roasting tin over the heat to loosen the debris from its base. Whisk in the flour and then pour in the stock you have made. Keep stirring until all is blended and thickened. Leave to cook over a very low heat for 5–10 minutes to ensure the flour flavour is cooked out. Add a little water from the brussels sprouts or any other vegetable if you think it is too thick. Check the seasoning, then strain it into a hot sauce-boat.

To cook the turkey: preheat the oven to Gas Mark 7/220°C/425°F. Stuff the turkey under its skin and in the neck; put the moisture-producing fruit and onion inside the bird. Rub a little oil or butter all over the skin. Put the bird on to one side in a roasting tin and roast it for 10 minutes. Turn it on to the other side and cook for another 10 minutes. Reduce the heat to Gas Mark 4/180°C/350°F and cook for 12 minutes per 500 g (1 lb), turning the bird to its other side just once. Small birds (up to 4.5 kg/10 lb) may require slightly longer per 500 g (1 lb), a bigger bird slightly less. Check by pushing a skewer into the thick part of the leg and also checking the juices inside the cavity; neither should show any pink in the juices whatsoever.

To turn the turkey safely take the roasting tin out of the oven and close the door quickly. Have an oven glove on both hands. Put the fingers of one hand in the cavity and firmly grab the pointed end of the rib cage. The other hand cups the part of the breast which is lying on the tin. Turn in stages. Don't worry if the skin breaks, as the stuffing protects the breast; but if a lot of flesh is exposed this is the time to baste generously. Put the turkey back into the oven and continue the cooking time per 500 g (1 lb) from that time. If the neck stuffing or any other part of the bird appears to be browing too quickly, use a loose tent of foil over that part only – never seal the roasting tin.

Once the bird is cooked it must rest for 30

minutes, and longer is better. Even birds of only 3 kg (7 lb) will stay piping hot for 30 minutes if they are not cut. The bird should be rested on its side and turned once, or rested on its breast (which keeps the moisture in the flesh rather than dropping into the body cavity). Prop a large bird on uncooked vegetables under its wings, so its weight does not squash the breast whilst resting.

For big numbers, carving is very much faster and easier if the whole of each side of the breast is taken off and sliced at an angle. Follow the instructions for taking off an uncooked breast on page 60 (Turkey Breasts in a Chestnut Overcoat).

Pictured on pages 4/5 and the front cover

GEORGIAN TURKEY FRICASSEE

Serves 6

Preparation time: 20 minutes + 45–60 minutes cooking + 30 minutes standing

- *1 kg (2 lb) lean cubed turkey, thawed if frozen*
- *600 ml (1 pint) chicken stock*
- *1/2 lemon, quartered*
- *1 sprig of fresh thyme*
- *3 egg yolks*
- *1 tablespoon sherry vinegar*
- *1 tablespoon anchovy essence*
- *1/2 teaspoon ground mace*
- *142 ml (1/4 pint) carton of double cream*

One of the most popular party dishes I have ever served. It does need to be finished with care at the last moment, but its authentic eighteenth-century Georgian savoury-creaminess is just right for those who believe the holiday season is a time for reflection and appreciation of the past. Don't mention the vinegar and anchovy essence unless you are asked. You can substitute chicken, rabbit or veal for the turkey.

Put the turkey and stock into a large, heavy-bottomed saucepan and slowly bring to the boil. Reduce the heat to its lowest and use a ladle and small sieve to remove any scum that forms. Add the lemon and thyme. Simmer very gently until the turkey cubes are tender, 45–60 minutes.

Pour off and finely strain as much of the liquid as you can. Squash the lemon pieces against the saucepan side to release the juices, then discard what is left of them.

Whisk the egg yolks with some of the hot liquid and reserve. Add the vinegar, anchovy essence and mace to the remaining liquid, then pour it back on to the turkey. It can sit like this, improving in flavour with no heat underneath it, for quite some time; a minimum of 30 minutes is good, giving you time to prepare or cook the accompaniments.

Pour in the egg mixture, place the pan over a low heat and stir gently until it starts to thicken. Add the cream and allow to thicken again. Err on the side of caution or you will have scrambled eggs. Serve with rice or a lot of potatoes, and green peas, a Georgian favourite with fricassees of all kinds.

Pictured on page 21

RIB OF BEEF WITH PICKLED WALNUT, WILD MUSHROOM AND PARSLEY STUFFING

Serves 8

Preparation time: 40 minutes + soaking walnuts + 2–3 hours cooking

Beef has been a celebratory British tradition for centuries longer than has turkey. Here sweet beef on the bone is teamed with old-fashioned pickled walnuts, rich wild mushrooms and fresh herbs to make a bright green tunnel of flavour in the middle of pink beef. Very festive.

1 rib beef roast, weighing about 3.5 kg (8 lb)

For the stuffing:

2 × 10 g packet of dried porcini mushrooms

300 g (10 oz) bottle of pickled walnuts

150 ml (1/4 pint) cream sherry

125 g (4 oz) fresh white breadcrumbs

50 g (2 oz) fresh parsley, chopped

15 g (1/2 oz) fresh thyme, chopped

3 garlic cloves, chopped

pepper

Rinse the porcini in running water, then cover them with water and heat slowly until reconstituted and tender. Rinse the pickled walnuts in running water, drain, then soak them in the sherry for several hours. Preheat the oven to Gas Mark 4/180°C/350°F.

To make the stuffing, toss the breadcrumbs with the herbs and garlic; season with pepper. Drain the walnuts and reserve the sherry. Set aside a whole walnut for every 2 guests. Lightly crumble the remainder and add them to the stuffing. Drain the mushrooms, reserving the soaking liquid, and stir them in; combine the liquid from the mushrooms with the sherry and reserve it. The walnuts you have saved may be kept in this liquid. Use a clean knife sharpener or wooden spoon handle to make an even tunnel through the centre of the meat. Push the stuffing in from either end, ensuring it meets in the

Rib of Beef with Pickled Walnut, Wild Mushroom and Parsley Stuffing

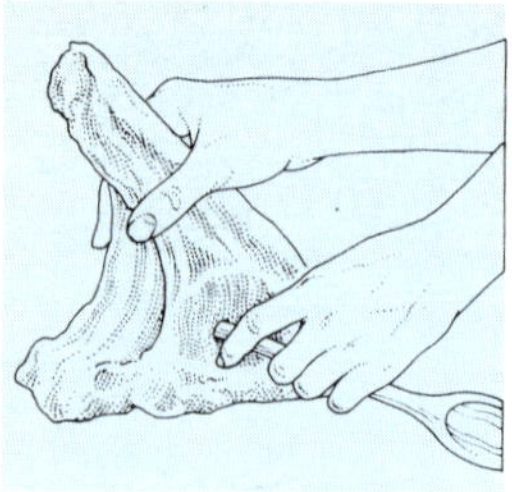

middle.

Roast the meat according to the accompanying instructions or to taste, allowing 10–20 minutes per pound plus 20 minutes, depending on how you like your beef. Ensure you leave at least 15 minutes for the meat to rest before carving it. While it rests, pour away most of the fat from the tin, then stir in the reserved mushroom/sherry liquid and bring to the boil. Once the juice is fully amalgamated and slightly syrupy, strain it into a hot jug. If you prefer rather more juice, add 300 ml (1/2 pint) of veal stock to the pan and boil everything together. If you like a thicker sauce, slake a teaspoon of cornflour with a tablespoon of the liquid and add slowly, stirring all the time until the texture is as you want it.

Serve in rather thick slices with a halved pickled walnut on each pool of sauce.

BEEF, ONION AND GUINNESS STEW

Serves 4–6

Preparation time: frying onions + 25 minutes + 2 hours cooking

75 g (3 oz) butter

500 g (1 lb) onions, chopped finely

1 kg (2 lb) stewing steak, chopped into 5 cm (2-inch) cubes

2 tablespoons plain flour

300 ml (1/2 pint) beef stock or consommé

300 ml (1/2 pint) Guinness

2–3 teaspoons brown sugar (optional)

salt and pepper

This takes patience to make, for if you do not cook the onions long enough they will not have the natural sweetness to balance the flavour of the Guinness. The reward is spectacular savouriness that can be served as it is, under a pie crust or, of course, with oysters. If you like the combination of Guinness and oysters, stir in fresh or defrosted frozen oysters, just before serving; for pies, layer them on the stew before you put on a pastry topping. Smoked oysters are specially good. Drain the oil from them and combine it with the butter in which you cook the onions.

Melt half the butter and add the onions. Fry very gently for 30–45 minutes, stirring from time to time, until the onions are really soft and sweet but still pale and barely golden. They should almost be a purée. Turn up the heat and brown them evenly, stirring most of the time so they do not burn: it may take another 15 minutes to do properly. Toss the steak in the flour, then lightly season it. In a large pan, melt the remaining butter, then brown the meat well over a low heat for about 10 minutes.

Add the onions, swirling out the pan in which they have cooked with the stock or consommé, so all the browned pieces and fat are used. Add that liquid plus the Guinness, stir well, then simmer for about 2 hours until tender. Add a little brown sugar about half-way through the cooking if the flavour is too bitter.

Serve the stew with rather a lot of mashed potato.

GOLDEN GOOSE WITH TRADITIONAL SAGE AND ONION STUFFING

Serves 6–8

Preparation time: 35 minutes + 2½–3 hours cooking + 30 minutes standing

1 goose, weighing about 4.5 kg (10 lb), thawed if frozen

2 onions

1 large lemon

1 large cooking apple

1 garlic clove

For the stuffing:

750 g (1½ lb) onions, unpeeled

125 g (4 oz) cooking apple, peeled and grated

50 g (2 oz) butter, softened

250 g (8 oz) fresh white breadcrumbs

4 tablespoons chopped fresh parsley

1–2 tablespoons dried sage

goose liver, chopped finely

1 tablespoon seasoned flour

salt and pepper

Britons are rediscovering the goose, putting it back to its traditional place in the centre of celebratory tables. It eats well with winter's fruits and dried fruits as long as they are served rather sharp or spiced.

This is the classic way of serving goose: it does not falsely flavour the fat, which should be collected and used for frying and roasting potatoes. In this case some of the fat is used to cook the stuffing, reversing the old way, when drippings from the spit were thickened with bread. For the less traditional family, Blueberry Wild Rice Stuffing (page 47) is particularly good with goose. A giblet gravy can be made the same way as for turkey (page 19).

The richness of goose and its sauce means you should serve vegetables with assertive flavours. I would recommend a celeriac and parsley purée, braised fennel, peas or beans, and perhaps the Roasted Red Pepper Mousselines (page 11), without the watercress sauce.

First make the stuffing. It is vital to get the sweetest possible flavour from the onions. If you have the time, roast them slowly in their skins at the bottom of the oven for an hour or more until tender, when cooking something else; otherwise boil them in water until really tender.

For the gilding:

1 egg yolk

1/4 teaspoon saffron strands

2 tablespoons milk

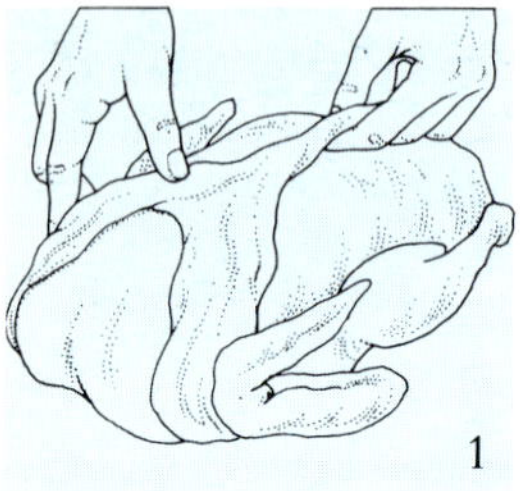

1

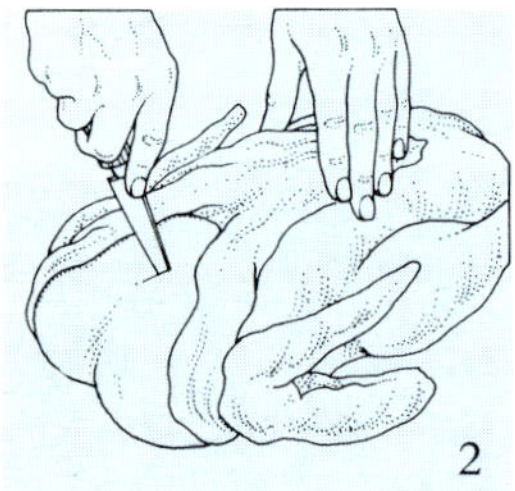

2

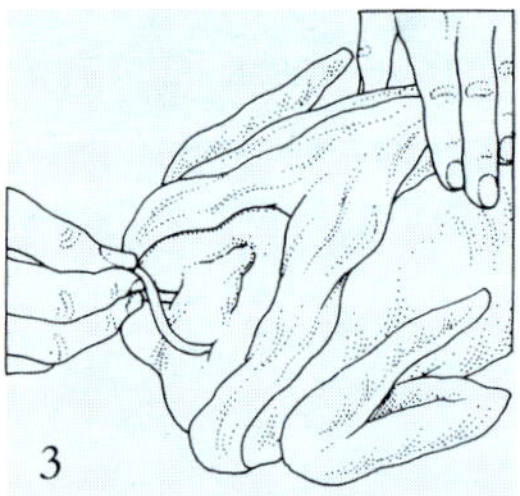

3

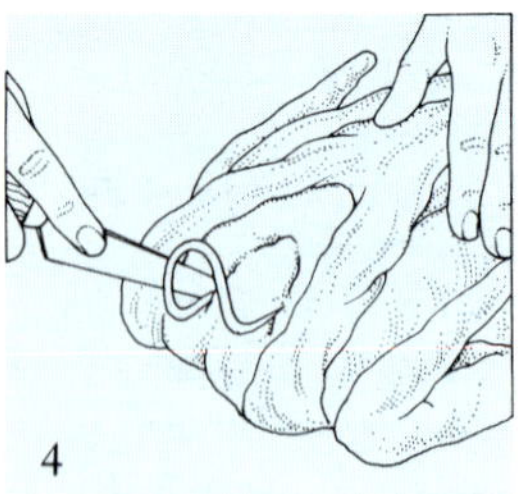

4

Peel and chop the cooked onion roughly while warm, and mix it with the apple and the butter. Toss lightly with the breadcrumbs. Season with salt and pepper and mix in the parsley and sage. Stir in the goose liver. The mixture should hold together when pressed lightly; if not, add a little milk or cream. Form the stuffing into small balls, then roll them in seasoned flour. An hour before the meal, collect a little of the fat from the roasting goose. Turn the stuffing balls in the fat then cook them in the oven for about 45 minutes until golden brown.

To cook the goose, preheat the oven to Gas Mark 4/350°C/180°F. Remove the giblets and all excess fat from inside the bird. Roughly chop or slice the onions, lemon and apple and put them inside the goose. Cut the garlic clove and rub it over the skin. Cut the wishbone out by turning back the neck flap to expose all the front of the breast (Fig. 1). With a small, sharp knife, cut down either side of the wings of the wishbone and behind the flange at the top (Fig. 2). Pull the released bone forward (Fig. 3) and then cut through the joints at the bottom of each side (Fig. 4). The cuts and any damage you make to the flesh disappear during the cooking, so don't worry if it looks rather untidy. If you are using a wild rice stuffing, push this into the neck end of the bird and pull the neck flap loosely around it, securing it with cocktail sticks.

Stand the bird on a rack in a roasting tin and cook it in the preheated oven for 15 minutes per 500 g (1 lb); this gives sweet, slightly pink flesh. Cook for another 30 minutes if you prefer the meat well done. Do not baste during cooking as this happens naturally, but do carefully ladle out excess fat if this is in danger of overflowing. Allow up to 20 minutes extra time for the bird to sit, lightly covered with foil, before you carve it. Pour off the excess fat and tip the juices from inside the bird into the pan, too. Discard the fruit and vegetables inside the bird. Note that with goose you do not have as much time after it has come out of the oven for other cooking, and so if you are roasting potatoes, for instance, they will have to start before the goose is removed.

When the bird comes out of the oven, mix the egg yolk, saffron and milk together and leave them in a warm place to develop flavour and colour. Just before serving, paint this gilding over the goose. Return the goose to the oven for 5 minutes so the gilding sets.

Serve the goose with the stuffing and giblet gravy if you've made it; also serve Cider Apple Sauce (page 50). Sit one or two Sweet-spiced Prunes (page 54) on the sauce. Kumquat Relish (page 54) is an excellent accompaniment and is best served hot.

Pictured on pages 48/9

BRAISED BARBARY DUCK WITH CRANBERRY RED CABBAGE

Preparation time: 20 minutes + 3–3½ hours cooking Serves 6

1 Barbary duck, weighing 2.75 kg (6 lb)

14 garlic cloves, unpeeled

2 bay leaves

500 g (1 lb) pickled red cabbage

125 g (4 oz) cranberries, thawed if frozen

1 tablespoon coriander seeds, crushed roughly

300 ml (½ pint) red wine

salt

Exceptionally easy to prepare. Goose with red cabbage is a traditional favourite in Scandinavian countries, but here a Barbary, the richest flavoured and fleshiest of ducks, is cooked on a bed of spiced red cabbage and red wine, so its juices add even more savour. Serve with Hackleback Potatoes (page 39) or a mash. The big gratifying flavour is too robust for wine, but chilled beer is just perfect.

Preheat the oven to Gas Mark 6/200°C/400°F. Cut off the tail of the duck and discard. Pull out any excess fat from the vent and reserve. Halve 2 of the garlic cloves and rub the cut edges over the skin of the duck, then put them inside with the bay leaves. Score the duck all over with a sharp knife.

Mix the remaining ingredients together and make a bed of them in an ovenproof dish, or roasting tin. Put the duck on to the bed of red cabbage, ensuring it is not sitting in the excess liquid. Cut up the reserved fat and put it around the duck. Cover with foil, making a high dome over the duck. Roast for 30–35 minutes per 500 g (1 lb), or according to directions. Half-way through the cooking time, remove the foil so the duck can brown. When cooked, place the duck on to a warmed dish to rest for at least 10 minutes. Drain the juices from the red cabbage mixture and boil them up rapidly for 5 minutes. Serve the duck quartered or sliced on a bed of red cabbage with a share of the garlic cloves, and pass the sauce around.

Pictured on pages 68/9

SALMON WITH DATE AND ALMOND STUFFING AND GINGER CRISPS

Serves 6

Preparation time: 30–45 minutes + 40 minutes cooking + 10 minutes standing

1 whole salmon, weighing 2 kg (4 1/2 lb)

175 g (6 oz) onions, sliced thinly

pepper

For the stuffing:

25 g (1 oz) long grain rice

50 g (2 oz) butter

25 g (1 oz) ground almonds

2 teaspoons sugar

1/2 teaspoon ground ginger

2 teaspoons ground cinnamon

18–24 fresh dates

For the ginger crisps:

a large, thick piece of fresh root ginger, about 15 cm (6 inches) long

2 tablespoons oil

This spectacular-looking fish dish is surprising to much modern taste, and although traditionally Islamic was once a great British favourite. Oliver Cromwell particularly enjoyed a version during Lent. You'll need a very big roasting tin to take a whole fish, and even so a 2 kg (4 1/2 lb) fish will probably be the biggest you can bake without problems. The alternative is to make a lipped baking shell of double foil on a flat baking sheet, but you must take great care not to pierce it and lose the delicious juices.

The gills and backbone of the salmon should be removed. These operations can be done at the fish counter, but give plenty of warning. If you are doing it, cut either side of the backbone, being careful not to pierce the skin (Fig. 1), open the fish out and cut the backbone out (Fig. 2). Remove the remaining bones from the sides with tweezers. Wash the fish in lightly salted water and dry.

Boil the rice until *al dente*, about 10 minutes. Drain it and mix it with the butter. When cold, mix in the almonds, sugar, ginger, and cinnamon. Slit the dates and remove the stones. Fill them with the rice mixture, pressing lightly.

Put the dates into the belly of the fish; there is no real need to sew or skewer the fish together when stuffed like this.

Preheat the oven to Gas Mark 5/190°C/375°F.

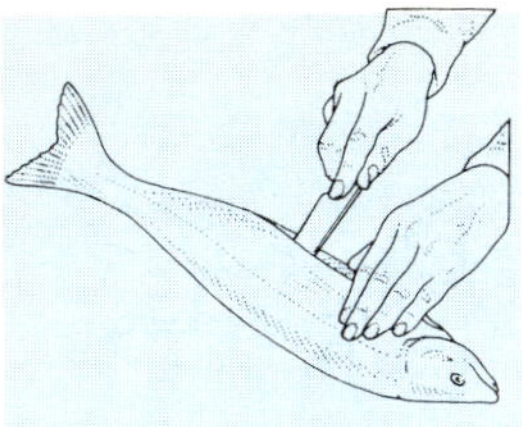

1

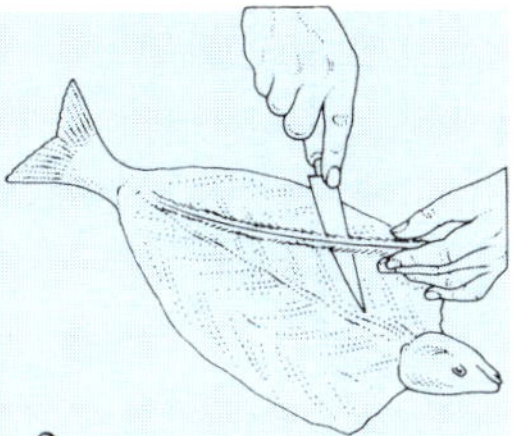

2

Put a strip of foil into the bottom of an ovenproof dish, ideally one from which the fish can be served, but probably in a roasting tin. Lay the fish on top of this. Scatter with the onion and a good deal of pepper. Add 200 ml (7 fl oz) of water and bake the fish for 20 minutes.

Remove the fish and turn up the temperature of the oven to Gas Mark 7/220°C/425°F. Use the strip of foil to turn the fish carefully on to its other side. Take the stuffed dates out of the cavity and arrange them around the fish. Add another 100 ml (3½ fl oz) of water to the roasting tin then baste the fish and the dates with the juices. Dust everything with more cinnamon. Bake for another 20 minutes, by which time the skin should be a pale golden colour and the small amount of juice should be lightly caramelised. Remove the fish from the oven and cover it loosely with a dome of foil for 10 minutes before serving. Cut everyone a thin strip of the top layer and a thin strip of the bottom layer and arrange them on hot plates, skin side up. Remove the skin from the bottom layer and spoon a little of the juices over the pink flesh. Put the dates on to this too.

To make the ginger crisps, peel the piece of ginger and then cut one end off diagonally. Use a vegetable peeler to cut long, thin slices from the diagonal face. Try to get 4 or 5 nice pieces per person. Heat a little oil in a pan and fry for about 3 minutes until crisp and brown, watching all the time, and turning frequently. Turn them quickly on to kitchen paper to drain. Serve scattered on the salmon.

Celeriac Mash (page 36) is just right with this.

Pictured on pages 44/5

SPINACH ROULADE WITH CHESTNUTS AND WILD RICE

Preparation time: 1 hour + 20 minutes cooking — Serves 6

This vegetarian dish is designed for occasions when only one or two of your guests don't eat meat and would be perfect for Christmas Day. Serve the vegetarians several

For the roulade:

500 g (1 lb) spinach, cooked, chopped and very well drained, juices retained

20 g (3/4 oz) butter, softened

1 tablespoon plain flour

3 eggs, separated

salt and pepper

For the filling:

125 g (4 oz) wild rice

1 1/2 × 350 g (12 oz) can of chestnuts

20 g (3/4 oz) butter

150 ml (1/4 pint) white wine

1 teaspoon ground nutmeg

1/2 teaspoon ground cinnamon

1/8 teaspoon ground cloves

For the sauce:

6 tablespoons Cranberry Sauce (page 51)

4 tablespoons white wine

2–4 teaspoons French mustard

slices of this hot festive roulade as their main course, and give everyone else a thin slice to enjoy with their turkey or other meat. The roulade is simple to make – marvellous cold too, as a buffet dish or first course.

Line a swiss roll tin, about 23 × 30 cm (9 × 12 inches) with baking parchment or buttered greaseproof paper. Trim to the upturned edges of the baking trays so there is no excess or overhang of paper. Doubly ensure the spinach is fully drained by turning it into a sieve and pressing hard with the back of a soup ladle. Add any juice to the other retained spinach juices. Cook the wild rice according to the packet instructions, using the spinach juice as the basis for the cooking liquid. Undercook it slightly so it retains a good chewiness. Blend or process two-thirds of the chestnuts with the butter, wine and spices, using a food processor or blender. Stir in the remaining chestnuts, roughly broken, and the cooked wild rice.

Preheat the oven to Gas Mark 5/190°C/375°F. To complete the roulade, stir the softened butter, flour, salt and pepper into the spinach. Beat the egg yolks lightly and add them too. Whisk the egg whites until firm but not stiff or dry. Stir a few tablespoons of the egg white into the spinach mixture, then fold in the remainder. Ladle the mixture into the prepared tin and gently ease into the edges and level out. Cook for 15–20 minutes. It should not brown and will feel evenly springy all over.

Turn the roulade on to a large sheet of greaseproof paper lying on top of a clean tea towel. Peel off the paper and spread the chestnut and rice mixture over it evenly. Make a line of cranberry sauce at the closest end to you, using 2 tablespoons of the sauce. Now use the paper and cloth to roll the roulade evenly. Tuck the paper and cloth around the shape to keep its form and keep it warm.

Make the sauce by boiling the remaining cranberry sauce, wine and mustard together for a few minutes until they have fully amalgamated. Serve with the roulade.

A Vegetarian Christmas Dinner: Grilled Aubergine and Chick-pea Mille Feuilles (page 34); Poached Mandarins with Cognac Ricotta (page 71).

WHISKY PIGEONS WITH BARLEY PILAFF

Preparation time: 20 minutes + 1 hour cooking Serves 4

- *4 pigeons*
- *4 streaky bacon rashers, chopped*
- *25 g (1 oz) butter*
- *125 ml (4 fl oz) malt whisky*
- *2 carrots, cut into sticks*
- *8 garlic cloves*
- *1 small onion, chopped*
- *450 ml (3/4 pint) red wine*
- *175 g (6 oz) pearl barley*
- *oil or butter for frying*
- *900 ml (1 1/2 pints) chicken or veal stock*
- *2 tablespoons chopped fresh parsley*
- *salt and pepper*

A terrific dish to serve for hogmanay. Blended whisky does not work as well as a single malt whisky. The recipe may be multiplied for larger numbers but the cooking time will not increase.

Preheat the oven to Gas Mark 3/160°C/325°F. Remove the back and legs from each bird, leaving the wings attached to the breast, which should now look rather heart-shaped. Discard the backs. Brown the bacon in the butter, then add the legs and breasts of the birds and brown well. Pour on half the malt whisky and flame, jiggling the pan until the flames subside. Add the carrots, garlic, onion and wine. Season lightly, transfer to an ovenproof dish, cover and braise in the oven for 1 hour or until tender.

Meanwhile, brown the barley in a little oil or butter, then add the stock and simmer uncovered for 25 minutes, stirring occasionally. Once cooked, add the parsley, stir well, cover and steam for 10 minutes before serving. Serve the breasts on a bed of buttery mashed swede. Make a border of the barley all round and pour the strained cooking juices on to that. Finally, drizzle a tablespoon of malt whisky over each of the breasts and serve at once.

Note: The backs would add further flavour to the cooking juices but they sometimes break up and make irritating inedible additions to the sauce. It's best to discard them at the start.

Pictured on pages 76/7

GRILLED AUBERGINE AND CHICK-PEA MILLE FEUILLES

Preparation time: 1 1/2 hours + 20–30 minutes cooking Serves 6

- *1 kg (2 lb) aubergines*
- *3 yellow peppers*
- *1 large fennel bulb*

This is a grand vegetarian meal for Christmas Day that is packed with bright colours and big modern flavours. It is properly balanced – not just vegetables – and so good that meat eaters have not realised it is vegetarian. There

2 tablespoons olive oil

2 × 432 g (14 oz) can of cooked chick-peas, drained

2 tablespoons tomato purée

25 g (1 oz) fresh parsley, chopped coarsely

25 g (1 oz) fresh mint, chopped coarsely

125 g (4 oz) feta cheese

270 g packet of filo pastry

250 g (8 oz) mozzarella cheese, sliced

2 tablespoons black olive pâté

50 g (2 oz) butter, melted

salt and pepper

are quite a number of steps but all may be done in advance and none is complicated.

Slice the aubergines diagonally about 1 cm (1/4 inch) thick – you need 24 slices approximately the same size. Sprinkle them with salt and place in a colander for 30 minutes, turning from time to time. Meanwhile, de-seed the yellow peppers and cut them from top to bottom to make the biggest slabs and rectangles you can from each. Trim off the inside ribs. Grill them under a medium heat for about 5 minutes until the skins have blistered and blackened. Cover the pepper pieces with a cloth for 15 minutes, then peel the skins away. Meanwhile, cut the fennel into 6 slices and poach them for 15–20 minutes until very tender. Drain well.

Rinse the aubergines well. Boil them for about 10 minutes until tender. Drain, and paint lightly with the olive oil. Grill both sides for 5–10 minutes on each side until golden, crisp and smelling rather sweet. Drain them. Place the chick-peas in a saucepan and stir in the tomato purée and chopped herbs. Cook over a low heat for about 2 minutes until the herbs have wilted. Remove from the heat, crumble in the feta cheese and season with plenty of pepper. Leave to cool.

Preheat the oven to Gas Mark 6/200°C/400°F. For each serving, brush 2 sheets of filo pastry with melted butter and stack them together; then cut each in half and put them on a lightly floured work surface. Distribute about two-thirds of the chick-peas in the centres of the pastry shapes. Construct the mille feuilles as follows: a layer each of aubergine, yellow pepper, aubergine, mozzarella cheese, olive pâté, aubergine, fennel, aubergine, then the remaining chick-pea mixture. Bring the sides of the pastry to the centre, then fold up the ends, brushing with melted butter. Bake the mille feuilles for 20–30 minutes until golden and crisp.

Pictured on page 33

ACCOMPANIMENTS AND VEGETABLES

ROAST POTATOES

Allowing 175–250 g (6–8 oz) per person, parboil the peeled potatoes for 10 minutes the day before you need them. Drain and cool them. Gently roughen the outsides with a fork. Cover and chill.

Preheat the oven to Gas Mark 5/190°C/375°F. To complete cooking, heat 1 cm (1/2 inch) lard or oil in a roasting tin, add the potatoes and turn them in the fat. Bake until cooking is completed and they are crisp and brown, turning them only once; the cooking time will vary from 30 to 45 minutes depending on the size of the potatoes, but can usually be done after the turkey comes out of the oven. Goose fat makes the best roast potatoes imaginable: pour off some of the fat the goose will make during cooking and use that: if the pan is big enough the potatoes may be cooked around the goose.

Pictured on pages 4/5

CELERIAC MASH

This purée reheats very well and so may be made in advance; in that case do not include the parsley but chop and stir some in just before serving. Many recipes include one-third or more potato, but it seems a shame to dilute the flavour. If you are not cooking the chopped celeriac immediately, cover it with acidulated water to prevent it from turning black.

Serves 6–8

1 kg (2 lb) celeriac, cut into small pieces

2 or 3 garlic cloves (optional)

50 g (2 oz) butter

about 100 ml (3 1/2 fl oz) milk

a handful of parsley

Cook the celeriac with the garlic (if using) in boiling salted water for 10–15 minutes, until tender. Drain and place in a food processor or blender. Add the butter and process, slowly adding milk to make a velvety texture. Add quite a lot of parsley and pulse it through, leaving it only roughly chopped.

Pictured on pages 4/5

BACON ROLLS AND CHIPOLATAS

Use unsmoked bacon, calculating 2 rolls per rasher. Trim off any rind and cut each rasher in half lengthways. Stretch each strip by pulling it against the back of a knife whilst holding it tight on a chopping board: roll tightly and put 2 or more rolls on to a cocktail stick. Bake slowly at the bottom of the oven, together with the chipolatas, for about 45 minutes. You can always turn up the oven and put them higher once the bird is out and resting.

Three chipolatas per person is generous, 2 is probably all most people want.

If you think either or both of these is a bit mundane for a festive meal, there are a number of things you can do:

Combine the two by wrapping the bacon around the chipolatas; it looks neater if the chipolatas are first cut in half.

Make little sausages of one or more of your stuffings and wrap the bacon around them.

Wrap the bacon around chestnuts if the latter are not appearing elsewhere on the plate. Do not bother to unthread the rolls; give the plates more festive interest by pushing the cocktail stick ends into a vegetable or the turkey, so they stand up.

Pictured on pages 4/5

BACON AND CHESTNUT SPROUTS

A good way to get the expectation of bacon and chestnuts out of the way so you can have more fun with the stuffings and vegetables: but serve these only if there are no bacon or chestnuts elsewhere on the plate. *Serves 6*

3 smoked streaky bacon rashers

50 g (2 oz) butter

2 or 3 cooked, peeled chestnuts

1/4 teaspoon freshly grated nutmeg

375 g (12 oz) brussels sprouts

Cut the bacon rashers into fine strips and cook them in the butter until lightly browned before you cook the sprouts. Add the chestnuts and nutmeg. Add the sprouts the moment they are ready, mix gently and serve.

SHERRY GINGER SPROUTS

An oriental tang to brighten up a plate of plainer-tasting vegetables. *Serves 6*

50 g (2 oz) butter

1 garlic clove, chopped

2.5 cm (1 inch) piece of fresh root ginger, grated

6 tablespoons dry sherry

375 g (12 oz) brussels sprouts, cooked

grated zest of 1/2 small orange (optional)

Melt the butter and add the garlic and ginger. Cook for 1 minute, then add the sherry. Turn up the heat and boil for 4–5 minutes until the liquid has reduced to a buttery syrup. Keep hot until you add the sprouts. Mix and serve. This is extra-good with the zest of orange grated into the sauce just before you add the sprouts.

ROASTED PARSNIPS

These are better with goose than with turkey, and better mashed than roasted with both. I combine both methods by roughly puréeing roasted parsnips with cream, lemon juice and parsley, keeping it roughly textured. First you still have to roast them, of course. Halve or quarter them lengthways; allowing up to 175 g (6 oz) per person. Put them into hot fat and then into the oven the moment the turkey comes out. They can be cooked with the potatoes.

POACHED CUCUMBER WITH ARTICHOKES

Poached cucumber was once a very popular vegetable and it is particularly good with turkey. It is a real treat combined with sliced artichoke hearts or bottoms, a common thing in Georgian times. *Serves 6*

1 large cucumber

400 g (13 oz) can of artichoke hearts or bottoms in brine

150 ml (1/4 pint) veal stock or double cream

salt and pepper

Peel the cucumber, then slice it in half lengthwise. Scoop out the seeds, then cut across each piece to make slices about 1 cm (1/2 inch) wide. Cook them in boiling water for 3 minutes or until just beginning to soften. Drain and cool them under running water, which encourages a bright colour. Drain and rinse the artichokes and slice them thickly. Heat the 2 vegetables through in the seasoned veal stock or cream.

Pictured on page 21

SWEET POTATO WITH PECANS

Substituting rum and nutmeg for the orange juice and cinnamon gives a decidedly Caribbean flavour.

Serves 6–8

1 kg (2 lb) sweet potatoes, peeled

150 ml (1/4 pint) fresh orange juice

1–2 teaspoons ground cinnamon

50 g (2 oz) butter, softened

100 g (3 1/2 oz) pecan nuts

1–4 tablespoons dark brown soft sugar (optional)

Slice the sweet potatoes thickly and lay them slightly overlapping in a single layer in a shallow ovenproof dish. Pour on the orange juice and scatter with the pecan nuts. If you like sweetness, add up to 4 tablespoons of dark brown sugar. Bake for 45–55 minutes at Gas Mark 4/180°C /350°F, until glazed and browning at the edges, basting once or twice. They will cook in the oven after the turkey is removed but may be finished under the grill.

Pictured on pages 16/17

SUCCOTASH

500 g (1 lb) frozen baby broad beans, thawed

500 g (1 lb) frozen sweetcorn

Remove the tough pale green outer skins from the beans. Cook the sweetcorn according to the packet instructions, and then mix in the beans and cook for another 2–3 minutes. The Succotash may be lightly buttered to serve; garlic butter gives extra flavour to the mixture. *Serves 6*

Pictured on pages 16/17

GREEN BEANS WITH GINGER

Allow 50 g (2 oz) per person. Top and tail the beans and boil them, only until they are bright green and still slightly crisp. Drain, toss them in a very little butter, then flavour the beans by grating fresh root ginger directly on to them.

Pictured on pages 16/17

TOMATO-CHILLI BAKED PUMPKIN

750 g (1 1/2 lb) pumpkin, de-seeded and cut in 2 cm (3/4-inch) slices or rings

4 tablespoons vegetable oil

397 g (14 oz) can of chopped tomatoes

4 garlic cloves, sliced thinly

1 tablespoon paprika

2–3 fresh green chillies, de-seeded and sliced thinly

142 ml (1/4 pint) carton of fresh soured cream

1 heaped teaspoon cumin seeds, roasted

1–2 tablespoons roughly torn fresh coriander, to garnish

Preheat the oven to Gas Mark 4/180°C/ 350°F. Leave the pumpkin in its skin and arrange the slices slightly overlapping in a shallow ovenproof dish. Sprinkle them with the oil. Mix together the chopped tomatoes, garlic, paprika and chillies. Pour over the pumpkin and bake for 45 minutes or until tender. Dot the soured cream on the cooked pumpkin and then scatter on the cumin seeds. Garnish with roughly torn fresh coriander leaves.

Serves 6–8

Pictured on pages 16/17

GRATIN OF TARRAGON COURGETTES

This is a mixture of Old and New World flavours. It's best warm rather than hot, so bake it early and then leave to one side.

Serves 6

1 kg (2 lb) courgettes, grated coarsely or sliced very thinly

1 tablespoon salt

40 g (1 1/2 oz) unsalted butter

125 g (4 oz) full-fat cream cheese

20 g (3/4 oz) Gruyère cheese, grated

1 tablespoon fresh tarragon leaves, chopped roughly, or 1 teaspoon dried tarragon

1/2 teaspoon grated nutmeg

75 g (3 oz) dried white breadcrumbs

50 g (2 oz) pine kernels

25 g (1 oz) parmesan cheese, grated

salt and pepper

Place the courgettes in a colander, sprinkle with the salt and leave to drain for 30 minutes. Rinse, drain and pat dry in a tea towel. Fry the courgettes in the butter for 3–4 minutes, stirring continuously. Mix in the cream cheese with the Gruyère, tarragon and nutmeg; season lightly with salt and pepper. Put the mixture into a ovenproof dish no bigger than 18 cm (7 inches) round or square. Mix the breadcrumbs, pine kernels and parmesan cheese and scatter on top. Bake the gratin for 20 minutes at Gas Mark 4/180°C/350°F. If it's not browned and crisp by then, finish it under a medium grill.

Pictured on pages 16/17

HACKLEBACK POTATOES

Otherwise known by the Swedish name of 'hasselback', these potatoes make a terrific alternative to plain roasted potatoes. They are a bit of a fiddle but turn a plain food into fun and make people smile.

Choose evenly sized potatoes of an oval shape. Peel and cut a thin slice from one of the narrow edges so that each potato sits up nicely. Using a sharp, thin-bladed knife, make cuts from the top to about three-quarters of the way down. They may be as close as you can manage or dare.

Preheat the oven to Gas Mark 5/190°C/375°F. Turn the potatoes in hot melted butter (2 tablespoons for 6 potatoes) in a roasting tin and then bake them for about an hour. You may have to start them before the turkey comes out if they are for the big day. Once cooked they may be further flavoured by basting them with garlic butter.

Pictured on pages 68/9 and the front cover

STUFFINGS AND SAVOURY SAUCES

BREAD-BASED STUFFINGS

Bread-based stuffings are not traditional in turkeys, geese or in any other poultry. Bread was used only to thicken the juices which dribbled from the basting of spit-roasted birds. When closed ovens replaced spits, many cooks re-created this delicious idea by putting flavoured breadcrumbs inside birds. But this method dangerously prevents the bird from cooking properly and also draws juices from the flesh, drying it. Thus, only fatty stuffings should touch the bird in either the neck flap or between the skin and the breast flesh.

Bread stuffings are best made into small balls and cooked in the roasting fats, much of which they will absorb to give even better flavour than stuffings put inside birds.

BASIC PORK STUFFING

Preparation time: 5 minutes

500 g (1 lb) coarse uncooked pork sausage, e.g. Toulouse or bratwurst, skinned or 500 g (1 lb) streaky pork rashers, chopped coarsely

125 g (4 oz) pork sausage meat

1 teaspoon dried thyme

1 teaspoon ground cinnamon

1/2 teaspoon ground nutmeg

1/4 teaspoon ground cloves

1 tablespoon finely chopped onion

1 teaspoon salt

This recipe makes a good amount of stuffing for a large 3.5–4.5 kg (8–10 lb) chicken or small turkey. Multiply it by two, three or four times for a larger turkey. The fat melts during cooking to baste the flesh beneath the skin, so you don't have to bother.

Mix all the ingredients together, using your fingers. Then add any of the following.

• VARIATIONS •

PRUNES, PORT AND WALNUT

125 g (4 oz) prunes, pitted and sliced roughly

4 tablespoons ruby port

50 g (2 oz) toasted walnuts, chopped roughly

Soak the prunes in the port for a few hours. Stir them into the basic mixture with the walnuts.

CELERY AND HAZELNUTS

2 tablespoons chopped celery leaves

125 g (4 oz) hazelnuts, toasted and chopped roughly

Mix the ingredients into the basic stuffing and combine well together.

Prunes, Port and Walnut Stuffing

CHESTNUT AND CRANBERRY

The cranberries explode slightly, looking wonderfully festive. Add only the cranberries or only the chestnuts if either is to feature elsewhere in the meal.

250 g (8 oz) unsweetened chestnut purée

250 g (8 oz) canned chestnuts, chopped roughly

3 tablespoons cognac

3-4 tablespoons cranberries, thawed if frozen

Mix the purée in very well, then fold in the remaining ingredients.

APRICOT AND MINT

One of the most popular recipes I have ever given on television and already a tradition in thousands of families. The combination of apricot with mint is essentially Eastern Mediterranean and thus very appropriate at Christmas.

125 g (4 oz) ready-to-eat dried apricots, sliced

grated zest of 1 small orange

1 heaped teaspoon dried mint

2-3 tablespoons cognac (optional)

Mix the ingredients thoroughly into the basic mixture.

BLACK CHERRIES, RUM AND PECANS

175 g (6 oz) canned black cherries, drained, pitted and halved

2 tablespoons dark rum

50 g (2 oz) pecans, toasted and crushed roughly

Soak the cherries in the rum for a few hours, then combine with any excess rum into the basic stuffing. Mix in the pecans.

BREAD SAUCE

Preparation time: 45 minutes + 2 hours standing | Serves 8

600 ml (1 pint) milk

1 large onion, quartered

2 mace blades

12 peppercorns

1 bay leaf

25 g (1 oz) parsley sprigs

1 celery stick with leaves, chopped

125 g (4 oz) fresh white breadcrumbs

2 tablespoons soured cream, greek-style yogurt, or double cream

a pinch of ground mace, to taste

a pinch of chilli powder, to taste

20 g (3/4 oz) butter

This is uniquely British and seems to have emerged in the early nineteenth century. Previously many sauces were thickened with bread but highly spiced, or finished the medieval way with vinegar; Mrs Beeton suggested thickening giblet stock with bread. Think of bread sauce as a savoury, slightly spiced white sauce and then you will get the flavour and the smooth shiny texture right; it should not be a thick bland blob. Take time to flavour the milk highly and you will be rewarded. I use soured cream or yogurt to finish the sauce as the slight sharpness is closer to the bite of the unpasteurised cream of traditional kitchens, but you can use double cream instead.

Place the milk, onion, mace blades, peppercorns, bay leaf, parsley and celery in a pan. Bring very slowly to the boil, then cover and simmer for 5 minutes. Remove the pan from the heat and allow to stand for at least 2 hours.

Strain the milk through a sieve, return it to the pan and stir in the breadcrumbs. Place the pan over a very low heat, stirring from time to time until the crumbs have swollen evenly, 20 minutes or so depending on the bread. Beat well to ensure an even texture and leave the sauce in a warm place; press some buttered greaseproof paper on the surface to stop a skin forming. When ready to serve, reheat the sauce and, beat in the soured cream, yogurt or cream, adding extra if the sauce is too thick, then stir in the ground mace and chilli powder to make a distinction from other flavours on the plate. Just before serving, whisk in the butter to polish and shine the sauce.

Pictured on pages 4/5 and the front cover

A Selection of Dishes with an Historical Influence: Salmon with Date and Almond Stuffing and Ginger Crisps (page 30), with Celeriac Mash (page 36); Fragrant Chicken and Almond Pie (page 55); Orange Mincemeat Meringue Tart (page 71); Dried Fruit Compôte with Rose-water and Almonds (page 80).

CURD CHEESE STUFFINGS

These rely on butter, the moisture of vegetables and the fat of curd cheese to baste the poultry flesh. They are much lighter and more fragrant than traditional, meat-based stuffings. It is very important that the ingredients are cool when mixed with the curd cheese. The following quantities are suitable for large 3.5–4.5 kg (8–10 lb) chickens or small turkeys; double or treble the quantities for larger turkeys.

• VARIATIONS •

LEEK WITH TOMATO AND MUSTARD

500 g (1 lb) leeks, sliced finely

284 ml (1/2 pint) carton of single cream

125 g (4 oz) butter

1 heaped tablespoon coarse-grain mustard

2 teaspoons tomato purée

375 g (12 oz) curd cheese

Cook the leeks over a gentle heat in the cream and butter for 15–20 minutes until soft. Reserve a quarter of the leeks and purée the rest with all the cooking liquid. Stir in the mustard, tomato purée and reserved leeks and allow to cool. Fold the mixture into the curd cheese.

HOT CARROT WITH CORIANDER STUFFING

This is brightly coloured and fashionably flavoured with coriander leaf. You can use parsley if you would rather. The small amount of fresh breadcrumbs keeps the stuffing firm enough to use but will not affect the moistness of the flesh.

500 g (1lb) carrots, grated coarsely

284 ml (1/2 pint) carton of single cream

125 g (4 oz) butter

375 g (12 oz) curd cheese

50 g (2 oz) fresh white breadcrumbs

1/2 teaspoon harissa or other hot chilli sauce, or to taste

2 tablespoons chopped fresh coriander

Cook the carrot in the cream and butter until really soft. Purée this and allow it to cool. Fold it into the curd cheese with the breadcrumbs, harissa or chilli sauce and coriander.

COURGETTE AND TARRAGON

500 g (1 lb) courgettes, grated coarsely

125 g (4 oz) butter

2 teaspoons dried tarragon

1 tablespoon creamed horseradish

1 tablespoon lemon juice

1/2 teaspoon pepper

1/4 teaspoon grated nutmeg

375 g (12 oz) curd cheese

salt

Sprinkle the courgettes with plenty of salt and allow to drain in a colander for 30 minutes. Rinse them well in running water, then squeeze them hard to dry as much as possible. Melt the butter and cook the courgettes in it for a few minutes. They will be a brighter colour and have absorbed some of the butter. Allow to cool. Stir in the flavourings and fold into the cheese.

BLUEBERRY WILD RICE STUFFING

Preparation time: 15 minutes + 40 minutes cooking

125 g (4 oz) wild rice

8 prunes, pitted and sliced thickly

2 tablespoons pecan nuts, toasted and cut in slices

2 heaped tablespoons fresh white breadcrumbs

2 tablespoons dark rum

1/2 teaspoon ground allspice

50 g (2 oz) butter, softened

225 g (7 1/2 oz) blueberries

Exotically flavoured, richly coloured, gorgeous contrasts of colour and texture based on ingredients from America – from where the turkey came. Use the stuffing with turkey or goose. This recipe makes enough to stuff a 3.5–4.5 kg (8–10 lb) bird, so multiply the quantities up as necessary. You could also try adding a 425 g (15 oz) can of pitted black cherries, instead of the blueberries.

Use this quite loose stuffing for the neck end of the bird. If you want to stuff the breast, increase the quantity of breadcrumbs to form a mixture that will slice easily when cooked.

Cook the wild rice in water for about 40 minutes until it is just beginning to soften. Drain well. Mix in the remaining ingredients, then add the blueberries. Pack the stuffing lightly into the neck end of the bird and fold the flap under, securing it with a cocktail stick. Do not do this too tightly because the rice will swell a little and may make the skin burst.

Pictured on pages 16/17

A Victorian-style Christmas Dinner: Golden Goose with Traditional Sage and Onion Stuffing (page 27), with Cider-Apple Sauce (page 50), Sweet-spiced Prunes (page 54) and Kumquat Relish (page 54).

CIDER APPLE SAUCE

Preparation time: 5 minutes + 25 minutes cooking | Serves 4

300 ml (1/2 pint) dry cider

500 g (1 lb) cooking apples, peeled, cored and sliced

2 teaspoons lemon juice

1 tablespoon chopped celery leaves

50 g (2 oz) butter, softened

Nutmeg may be added if you are not serving the Sweet-spiced Prunes (page 54). A little Calvados or cognac added at the end makes celebration more likely.

Place the cider in a pan and bring to the boil. Boil it vigorously for about 10 minutes until just a few tablespoonfuls remain. Add the apple to the saucepan with the lemon juice and celery leaves. Cover and cook over a medium heat for about 15 minutes, stirring occasionally, until a pulp. Strain through a sieve and beat in the butter.

SPICED RED CHERRY SAUCE

Preparation time: 30 minutes | Serves 4-6

300 ml (1/2 pint) red wine

150 ml (1/4 pint) ruby port

1 cinnamon stick

2 whole cloves

5 cm (2-inch) strip of orange zest

1 bay leaf

2 tablespoons cornflour

500 g (1 lb) red cherries, pitted or 420 g (14 oz) can of red cherries, pitted

a little sugar or redcurrant jelly (optional)

A terrific sauce with all birds, especially goose, but a great change with turkey on the big day. A few tablespoons of cognac or dark rum might be added, and a knob of butter.

Simmer the wine and port with the spices, orange zest and bay leaf for 10 minutes; then allow to stand for another 10 minutes. Strain and then return the wine to the saucepan. Mix a few spoonfuls of the liquid with the cornflour. Stir it in and heat slowly until the sauce thickens and clears. Add the cherries and heat thoroughly, stirring as you do so. The cherries will add extra colour and juice to the sauce, which will thin a little. Taste and sweeten it if you like with a little sugar or redcurrant jelly.

Pictured on page 53.

CRANBERRY SAUCES

Preparation time: 15 minutes | Serves 6-8

500 g (1 lb) cranberries, thawed if frozen

100–150 ml ($3^{1}/_{2}$–5 fl oz) water

1 cinnamon stick

175 g (6 oz) caster sugar

Cranberries make terrific sauces with almost anything else. There is only one rule. Never add the sugar until the berries are cooked or the skins will toughen and have to be puréed or sieved. All the sauces below are much better served hot. Once warmed through, the sauce may have all sorts of alcohol or juices stirred in to complement the other flavours with which you will serve it. The best additions are orange liqueurs, cognac, rum, red or white wine, apple or orange juice, and of all things, gin.

Put the cranberries into a saucepan with the water and cinnamon stick. Bring slowly to the boil, stirring from time to time, and cook for about 5 minutes until the skins begin to pop. Remove the pan from the heat, take out the cinnamon stick and stir in the sugar.

For a smooth sauce, cook the fruit for about 15 minutes until a pulp, remove the pan from the heat, take out the cinnamon stick, stir in the sugar and then sieve whilst still warm.

Pictured on pages 4/5 and the front cover

• VARIATIONS •

- Use orange, apple, pineapple, grape or other juice instead of water.
- Add 125 g (4 oz) of blueberries.
- Use red or white wine, port, vermouth, Madeira or sherry instead of water.
- Add a bay leaf and several cloves for a spicier savoury flavour.
- Use soft brown or demerara sugar instead of caster sugar.
- Use maple syrup instead of sugar.
- Add 50 g (2 oz) toasted and chopped pecans, walnuts or almonds to the completed sauce.
- Add 1 or 2 tablespoons blanched matchsticks of orange zest.

HOT MUSTARD CRANBERRY SAUCE

6 tablespoons Cranberry Sauce

4 tablespoons white wine

2 teaspoons Dijon mustard

Boil the ingredients together for 3–5 minutes, stirring all the time until blended. Heat reduces the bite of the mustard so you might want to stir in a little more before serving.

CRANBERRY RELISH

Makes about 750 g (1½ lb)

Preparation time: 15 minutes + 24 hours standing

1 large orange

1 small lemon

1 large cooking apple

250 g (8 oz) cranberries, thawed if frozen

125 g (4 oz) white or brown sugar, or to taste

This old East Coast American way with cranberries is quickly prepared and lasts weeks when refrigerated. A perfect relish with cold meats, pâtés and pies of every kind and a welcome and unusual Christmas present.

Wash the orange and lemon very well, quarter them and remove all pips. Core but do not peel the apple. Process the orange and lemon in a blender or food processor until roughly chopped; you may have to do this in several batches. Add the apple and chop roughly. Add the cranberries and process until the cranberries are cut up but remain different sizes. Tip everything into a bowl and add the sugar. Cover and leave at room temperature for 24 hours, then taste again. The relish will have begun to soften and blend. Add extra sugar if you like. Store for at least a week before using; longer is better. Kept in the refrigerator, the sauce will keep for up to four weeks.

• VARIATIONS •

Any or all of the following ingredients may be added:

- 50 g (2 oz) celery, chopped finely.
- 125 g (4 oz) fresh pineapple, chopped finely.
- 125 g (4 oz) pecans or walnuts, toasted and chopped.
- 2 or 3 tablespoons vodka, gin, cognac or port.

Spiced Red Cherry Sauce (page 50)

HOT KUMQUAT RELISH

Preparation time: 15 minutes + 50 minutes cooking | Serves 6–8

250 g (8 oz) kumquats

300 ml (1/2 pint) fresh orange juice

1 bay leaf

1 garlic clove (optional)

2 tablespoons caster sugar, or to taste

Bright orange kumquats have become one of the features of Christmas. This sharp-tasting, vibrantly coloured relish may be served hot or cold and makes a delicious contrast to the other sauces of the season. Serve it as well as cranberry sauce. An original and welcome gift too; it keeps for 6 weeks in the fridge.

Wash the kumquats thoroughly and then slice them lengthways into quarters and remove any pips. Put them in a saucepan with the orange juice, bay leaf and garlic if using. Simmer uncovered over a gentle heat until tender and looking rather transparent and the liquid is thick and syrupy, which may take up to 50 minutes. The syrup should almost have evaporated. Remove the bay leaf and garlic. Stir in the sugar. Serve hot or cold.

Pictured on pages 48/9

SWEET-SPICED PRUNES

Preparation time: 10 minutes + 1 1/4-1 1/2 hours cooking | Serves 12

24 large prunes

600 ml (1 pint) red wine

300 ml (1/2 pint) sweet sherry or port

3 bay leaves

2 cinnamon sticks

12 juniper berries

6 cardamom pods, split and lightly bruised

2 × 5 cm (2-inch) strips of lemon zest

2 tablespoons muscovado or dark brown soft sugar

Absolutely delicious served hot or cold with roast poultry and game, with goose, duck, lamb, ham and all cold meats. They keep for months refrigerated. Serve only 1 or 2 per person. Try ready-to-eat dried apricots or peaches instead of prunes, and white wine rather than red. A dash of Tabasco sauce in either is liked by many.

Put all the ingredients in a pan and simmer gently uncovered for 1 1/4-1 1/2 hours until the liquid is reduced to a thick syrup which just coats the prunes. Cool, then remove the lemon zest but leave the spices. Keep refrigerated.

Pictured on pages 48/9

FRAGRANT CHICKEN AND ALMOND PIE

Serves 8 or more

Preparation time: 1 hour + 45 minutes cooking + 20-30 minutes cooling

- *4 boneless chicken breasts, cooked*
- *175 g (6 oz) blanched almonds*
- *250 g (8 oz) butter*
- *4 tablespoons fresh lemon juice*
- *1/2 sachet of saffron strands*
- *8 tablespoons coarsely chopped fresh parsley*
- *9 large eggs (size 1-2)*
- *250 ml (8 fl oz) chicken stock*
- *6 teaspoons ground cinnamon*
- *2 teaspoons ground cumin*
- *1 tablespoon olive oil*
- *4 × 270 g packets of filo pastry*
- *2 tablespoons caster sugar*

Perfect for buffets or dinner parties, because it is best served lukewarm rather than straight from the oven. The pie has a subtle exotic flavour and is based on one of the Eastern Mediterranean's most famous dishes.

Pull or slice the chicken breasts into long generous pieces. Roast or toast the almonds thoroughly for about 10 minutes and then chop them roughly, leaving about half of them whole or almost so. Melt 175 g (6 oz) of the butter, and add the lemon juice and saffron. Remove the pan from the heat, add the chicken and the parsley and leave to cool, stirring from time to time.

In a saucepan, whisk the eggs with the chicken stock, cinnamon and cumin and cook until only just starting to set, about 8 minutes. Turn them into a bowl to stop the cooking.

Preheat the oven to Gas Mark 6/200°C/400°F. Melt the remaining butter with the olive oil. Use about two-thirds of the filo sheets to line the sides and edges of a deep baking dish, approximately 23 × 30 cm (9 × 12 inches), painting the pastry with the melted butter and oil mixture as you go. Leave a good overhang all round.

Sprinkle half the almonds on to the pastry, together with half the sugar. Spread on half the egg mixture and arrange the chicken pieces evenly over that. Pour over any butter or juices remaining. Cover with the remaining egg, then with the remaining almonds and sugar.

Turn in the excess pastry and then layer the remaining pastry on top, painting it with melted oil and butter. Use a very sharp knife to cut a diamond pattern through the top 4 layers or so of the filo pastry. Bake for 45 minutes or until you

A Buffet Party: Pheasant, Prune and Caramelised Chestnut Party Pie (page 58); Turkey Breasts in a Chestnut Overcoat (page 60); Ratafia Orange Cheesecake (page 62).

are sure all the pastry is well cooked through, crisp and golden. If some of the edges seem in danger of burning, spray or dab them with cold water. Leave to cool for 20–30 minutes before serving. It's also wonderful served cold, although the pastry is likely to lose some of its crispness.

Pictured on pages 44/5

PHEASANT, PRUNE AND CARAMELISED CHESTNUT PARTY PIE

Serves 16

Preparation time: 1¼ hours + 30 minutes marinating + 3 hours cooking

For the filling:

1 cock pheasant

350 ml (12 fl oz) port, Madeira or cream sherry

25 g (1 oz) butter

25 g (1 oz) sugar

2 teaspoons vinegar

125 g (4 oz) cooked peeled chestnuts

500 g (1 lb) minced pork

500 g (1 lb) minced veal

125 g (4 oz) smoked bacon, minced

2 teaspoons dried thyme

1 teaspoon ground nutmeg

1 teaspoon ground allspice

1 teaspoon salt

1 quantity Sweet-spiced Prunes (page 54)

1 tablespoon oil

2 × 24 g packets of aspic powder

For the pastry:

750 g (1½ lb) plain flour

A generously packed, cold raised pie is a fitting centrepiece of any festive buffet, but is also a very handy and long-lasting standby to have in a holiday kitchen.

Preheat the oven to Gas Mark 6/200°C/400°F. Clean the pheasant, removing every trace of feathers from the skin. Pull off the skin and any yellow fat and reserve them. Cut the breasts off the pheasant and slice each into 4 long strips. Put them into a shallow dish with 4 tablespoons of port, Madeira or sherry. Leave to marinate for 30 minutes.

Melt the butter and sugar together in a small pan over a medium heat, stirring occasionally, until a rich brown. Add the vinegar (carefully, it spits) and the chestnuts and toss until they are covered. Cool.

Finely process all the remaining flesh and reserved skin and fat from the pheasant in a food processor; reserve the carcass. Mix with the other minced meats, 4 tablespoons of the port, Madeira or sherry, the thyme, spices and salt. Lightly crush the caramelised chestnuts and stir them through, keeping the pieces relatively big.

Next make the pastry. Sieve the flour with the salt in a large mixing bowl and make a well in the centre. Heat the water and lard until the lard has melted, and pour into the flour. Mix well and knead until smooth. Use the pastry whilst still warm, pressing it into shape rather than rolling.

2 teaspoons salt

300 ml (1/2 pint) water

250 g (8 oz) lard, cut into small pieces

1/2 beaten egg, to glaze

Line a 25 cm (10-inch) greased, loose-bottomed or springform cake tin with three-quarters of the pastry. Ensure you do not have excess pastry where the sides join the bottom. Wrap the remainder and keep it warm. Cut the prunes in half, remove the stones, and use half the amount to make a layer on the pastry. Put in half the minced meat and make a layer of the strips of pheasant breast. Cover with the rest of the minced meat and make another layer of prunes.

Roll out a lid for the pie on a floured surface; seal and crimp the edges firmly and deeply. Slash the top and pull back the edges to ensure it stays open. Bake for 30 minutes, then reduce the temperature to Gas Mark 3/160°C/325°F and cook for another 2 1/2 hours, covering the pie loosely with foil if it's browning too quickly. After 1 hour, glaze the pie with the beaten egg.

Brown the pheasant bones in the oil, then cover with about 750 ml (1 1/4 pints) of water and simmer for 1 hour. Strain the liquid through a sieve, return it to the pan and reduce it over a high heat to 250 ml (8 fl oz). Dissolve the aspic in the warm stock and add the remaining port, Madeira or sherry. When the cooked pie is cool, pour the liquid through the top a little at a time and in several stages (this takes time and patience). Refrigerate and leave for several days before cutting.

TURKEY BREASTS IN A CHESTNUT OVERCOAT

Serves 6–8

Preparation time: 2 hours + 4 hours standing + 2¾ hours cooking

1 turkey, weighing 3 kg (7 lb)
5 tablespoons orange or mandarin liqueur
4 tablespoons ruby port
2 tablespoons oil
2 tablespoons plain flour
125 g (4 oz) onion, chopped coarsely
1 bay leaf
1 orange
1 celery stick, chopped finely
1 large sprig of fresh thyme
1 litre (2 pints) boiling water (or half water/half red wine)
200 g (7 oz) minced pork
50 g (2 oz) ground hazelnuts
1 teaspoon fresh thyme, chopped
2 tablespoons celery leaf, chopped coarsely
1 teaspoon cinnamon
1 teaspoon nutmeg
¼ teaspoon ground cloves
1½ × 350 g (12 oz) can of chestnuts
40 g (1½ oz) butter, melted
salt and pepper

A spectacular way to do all the work the day before: turkey breasts baked in a protective coating of their own dark meat with glazed chestnuts. Simple to carve too, so everyone enjoys the big day. Just as wonderful cold, so a tremendous centrepiece for buffets and summer picnics, too. This can also be made with a turkey breast joint and 750 g (1½ lb) of turkey mince.

Remove the giblets and put them to one side. Remove the skin from the turkey and discard it. Using a small, very sharp knife remove the two sides of the breast meat in single pieces. Start by slicing either side of the breast keel (Fig. 1), then follow the curve of the rib cage with the tip of the knife (Fig. 2). Put the 2 breasts into a shallow dish with 4 tablespoons of the orange liqueur and port and leave at room temperature for up to 4 hours, turning from time to time.

Remove all the dark meat from the carcass, legs and wings and put it to one side, with the heart and the liver from the giblets. Chop the carcass and brown it very well in the oil in a large saucepan, together with the neck and gizzard. Sprinkle in the flour. Add the onion, bay leaf, the peel of half the orange, the celery, and the thyme. Pour on the boiling water or water and wine. Cook gently for 2 hours, then strain the liquid into a bowl, return it to the pan and continue cooking, uncovered, for about 30 minutes until there is no more than 300 ml (½ pint) of rich turkey stock.

Purée the dark turkey meat with the heart and liver in a food processor or put it through a mincer several times using the finest blade. Mix it with the minced pork. On to that mixture grate the zest of the remaining half-orange, then add the hazelnuts, thyme, celery leaf, spices and half the chestnuts, plus any of the marinade that has not been absorbed. Mix very well with your

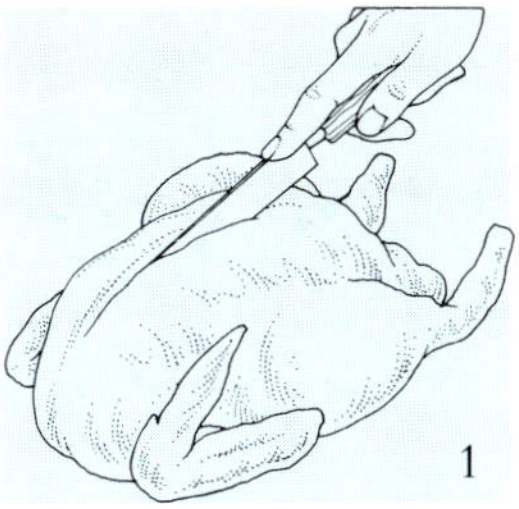

1

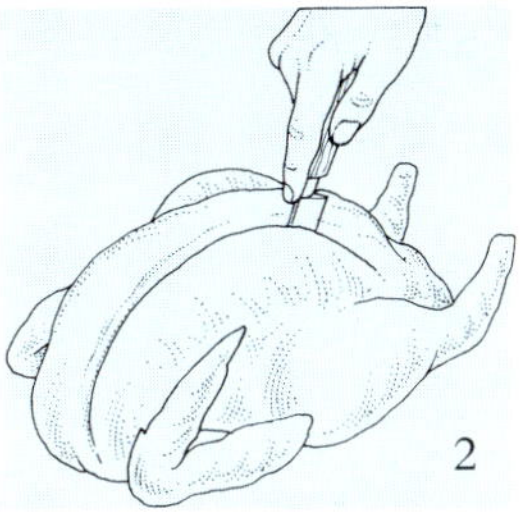

2

hands; you will find the stringy white leg tendons as you do so and these should be removed.

Preheat the oven to Gas Mark 6/200°C/400°F. Divide the mixture into 2 portions, one slightly smaller than the other. Halve the smaller portion and put both halves on a baking sheet. Flatten each to a shape slightly bigger than the breasts. Put a breast on top of each base, and lightly season with salt and pepper. Use the remaining mixture to coat the breasts entirely.

Sort 16 nice chestnut halves from those that remain and arrange 8 down the centre of each covered breast. Crumble the remaining chestnuts roughly and press them on to the outsides.

Bake for 60 minutes. Half-way through, paint the chestnuts with the melted butter mixed with the remaining 1 tablespoon of orange liqueur. Let the meat rest for 10 minutes after cooking before slicing quite thickly, between the chestnut halves. Taste the sauce and adjust the seasoning. Thicken slightly if you prefer. Also serve a cranberry sauce: Hot Mustard Cranberry Sauce (page 52) is very good with this.

Pictured on pages 56/7

SPICED HAM OR GAMMON WITH MADEIRA PEACH SAUCE

Serves 6-8

Preparation time: 10 minutes + 2 hours soaking + 1½ hours cooking + 20 minutes standing

1 joint of ham or gammon, weighing 1.5 kg (3½ lb)

1 cinnamon stick

6 cloves

2 mace blades

2 bay leaves

For the sauce:

411 g (14½ oz) can of chicken consommé

Soak the ham or gammon in cold water for 2 hours and drain. Cover it with fresh cold water and bring slowly to the boil, adding the spices and bay leaves. Cover and simmer very gently indeed for 25 minutes per 500 g (1 lb). Leave to stand in the liquid for at least 20 minutes before removing to slice. Meanwhile, boil the consommé until reduced by half.

Heat the sauce ingredients together for 4–5 minutes. Thicken if you like with a teaspoon of cornflour slaked with a tablespoon of the sauce. Add slowly, stirring as you do, until the

3 tablespoons peach jam, sieved

3 tablespoons Madeira

2 tablespoons lemon juice

To garnish:

411 g (14½ oz) can of peach halves in natural juice

15 g (½ oz) butter

¼ teaspoon freshly grated nutmeg

sauce has thickened to your preference.

Place the peach halves in a small ovenproof dish. Dot them with butter, sprinkle with nutmeg and grill them for about 5 minutes until golden brown. Serve with the sliced meat and sauce.

RATAFIA ORANGE CHEESECAKE

Preparation time: 10 minutes + 55–60 minutes cooking | Serves 16

For the base:

200 g (7 oz) ratafia biscuits, crushed finely

2 tablespoons caster sugar

25 g (1 oz) deluxe plain cooking chocolate, melted

125 g (4 oz) butter, melted

For the filling:

125 g (4 oz) white almond paste (marzipan)

4 tablespoons amaretto liqueur or apricot brandy

750 g (1½ lb) cream, curd or ricotta cheese

75 g (3 oz) caster sugar

4 eggs

grated zest of 2 oranges

100 g (3½ oz) cut mixed peel

284 ml (½ pint) carton of double cream

250 g (8 oz) ratafia biscuits, crushed coarsely

Almonds and oranges are two of the most common symbols of Christmas food. Here they are combined in an extraordinary cheesecake, almost too good to eat. Italian amaretti biscuits are an excellent substitute for the ratafias, if you have been given some. It must be made the day before you need it.

Combine the ingredients for the base and press firmly and evenly into the base of a 23 cm (9-inch) springform or loose-based tin. Refrigerate.

Preheat the oven to Gas Mark 5/190°C/375°F. Break up the almond paste and beat in the liqueur. Beat the cheese and sugar together until smooth. Beat in the eggs one by one. Stir in the orange zest, mixed peel and cream. Fold in the ratafia biscuits. Ladle the filling into the prepared tin and bake for 55-60 minutes. It will seem soft but firms as it cools. Allow to cool completely, then refrigerate overnight. Serve in very thin slices, perhaps with the Dried Fruit Compôte (page 80).

Pictured on pages 56/7

TOFFEE-APPLE AND WALNUT PIE

Serves 8

Preparation time: 30 minutes + 20 minutes standing + 1 hour cooking

For the pastry:

400 g (13 oz) self-raising flour

150 g (5 oz) caster sugar

a few drops of vanilla essence

1 egg

2 teaspoons milk

200 g (7 oz) unsalted butter

For the filling:

200 g (7 oz) walnut pieces, toasted

grated zest of 1 small orange

1 kg (2 lb) Golden Delicious apples, peeled, cored and quartered

1 teaspoon ground cinnamon

75 g (3 oz) butter

250 g (8 oz) caster sugar

2 tablespoons fresh orange juice

A wonderful pie for entertaining, gorgeously flavoured and a little gooey.

Preheat the oven to Gas Mark 4/180°C/350°F. Sieve half the flour on to a clean cool surface and make a well in the centre. Mix together the sugar, vanilla, egg and milk; put them in the well, then mix with the flour. Rub the butter into the remaining flour, then knead the 2 mixtures into an even dough. Let it rest in the refrigerator for at least 20 minutes.

Use half the dough to line the base only of a 23 cm (9-inch) springform or loose-bottomed cake tin, prick it all over and bake for 15–20 minutes. Let it cool.

Roll out the remaining pastry rather thinly and cut a lid for the springform pan or cake tin. Use the leftover pastry to line the side of the pan, pressing it in piece by piece and ensuring a good seal with the base. Grind half the toasted walnuts, add the orange zest and put most of this mixture on to the pastry base. Arrange the apple pieces as tightly as you can, adding in the remaining ground walnuts and the walnut pieces. Sprinkle on the ground cinnamon. Heat the butter and sugar gently in a small pan to make a rich dark caramel, cooking courageously until you smell the first hint of burning. Remove from the heat, add the orange juice, swirl round and immediately pour evenly over the apples.

Put on the pie top and seal it all round. Make 4 long slashes, brush the pastry with milk and bake it for 60 minutes. Let the pie cool completely in the tin before taking it out, preferably overnight.

The pastry may be crispened again without any need to heat all the pie; bake for about 15 minutes at Gas Mark 4/180°C/350°F. Cool before serving.

Pictured on page 93

FILO MINCEMEAT TRIANGLES AND CRACKERS

Preparation time: 1 hour + 10-15 minutes cooking — Makes 36

6 sheets of filo pastry, thawed if frozen

75 g (3 oz) unsalted butter, melted

1 quantity Improved Christmas Mincemeat (page 92)

icing sugar, to decorate (optional)

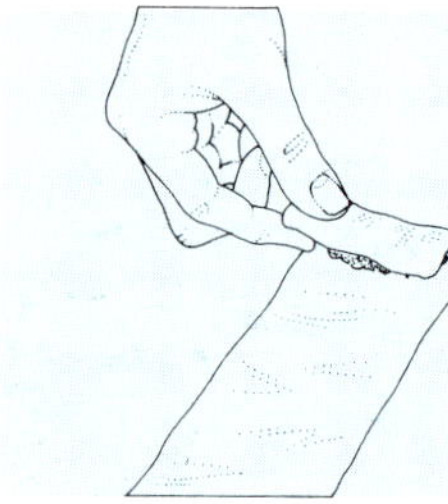

1

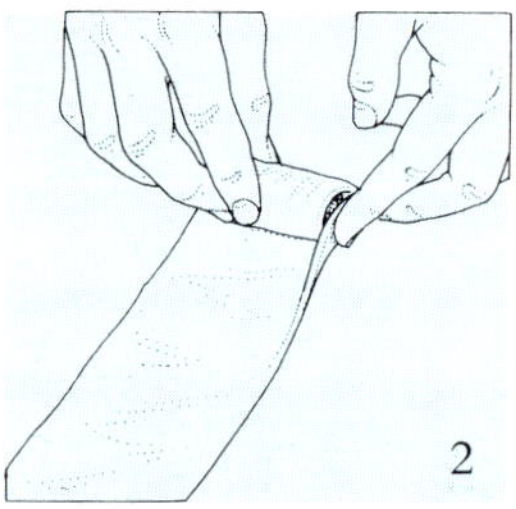

2

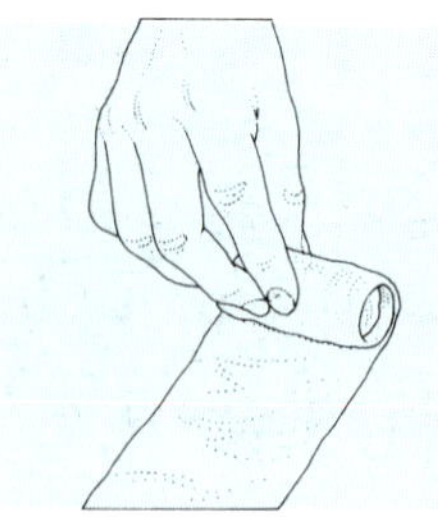

3

These look complicated and special but are very simple to make and need no special baking sheets or pie dishes.

Put the pastry on a board with the long side towards you. Measure 8 cm (3-inch) intervals, which will give 6 strips. Use a long sharp knife to cut through the pastry at these marks, giving 36 strips. If you have the time and patience, you can cut 12 strips, which make smaller shapes that are far easier to eat if guests are standing.

Paint the top layer with the melted butter. Put about 1 teaspoon of mincemeat at the end closest to you; this amount may have to be adjusted.

To make triangles: pick up the right-hand corner and take it diagonally to the left-hand side of the pastry, so the fold forms a neat triangle enclosing the filling. Fold that straight up and then fold over to the right-hand long side. Continue like this and by the time you reach the end the filling will be neatly enclosed. Make sure, though, that you do not roll or fold the triangles too tightly.

To make crackers: form the mincemeat into a small roll across the end closest to you, but leave a space about as wide as your little finger each side. Roll the pastry once around the filling (Fig. 1) and then turn in the sides for about 5 cm (2 inches) (Fig. 2). Roll tightly until all the folded pastry is enclosed (Fig. 3), then roll the remainder of the pastry in a single continuous movement – if you can. The filling will be nicely enclosed but the ends will be open. Leave like this, which is the traditional shape, or twist slightly to make them look like crackers (Fig. 4).

Preheat the oven to Gas Mark 5/190°C/375°F. Lay the pastries on a baking sheet and bake for 10–15 minutes, until golden brown and nicely crisp. If made much in advance they will soften, but they can be rebaked; a quick spray of water

Filo Mincemeat Triangles and Crackers (page 64)

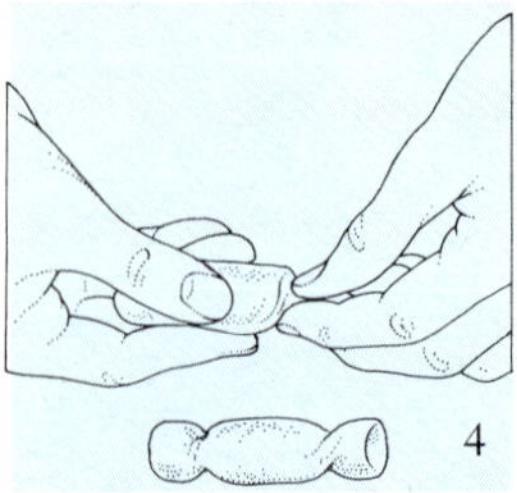

4

will stop the ends burning. If they will not be too sweet for you, it looks very nice to sieve a little icing sugar over the pastries just before serving.

DOUBLE CHOCOLATE RASPBERRY TRUFFLE CAKE

Preparation time: 30 minutes + overnight chilling — Serves 12

200 g (7 oz) deluxe plain cooking chocolate, broken into pieces

200 g (7 oz) unsalted butter, softened

200 g (7 oz) white chocolate, broken into pieces

100 g (3½ oz) ground walnuts

2 heaped tablespoons cocoa powder

2 tablespoons icing sugar

3 tablespoons cognac

100 g (3½ oz) ground almonds

½ teaspoon orange-flower water or rose-water

250 g (8 oz) raspberries, thawed if frozen

In a small saucepan, gently melt together the broken-up dark chocolate with half the butter; in another saucepan melt the white chocolate with the remaining butter.

To the dark chocolate mixture add the walnuts, 1 heaped tablespoon of cocoa, 1 tablespoon of the icing sugar and the cognac.

To the white chocolate mixture add the ground almonds, 1 tablespoon of icing sugar and the orange-flower or rose-water.

Purée the raspberries in a food processor or blender, and push them through a sieve using the back of a spoon. Line a 20 cm (8-inch) springform or loose-based cake tin with baking parchment or with clingfilm. Sprinkle lightly with the remaining heaped tablespoon of cocoa powder.

Swirl half the raspberries into the dark chocolate mixture and ladle it into the bottom of the tin. Swirl the remaining raspberries into the white chocolate mixture and ladle that carefully over the dark chocolate layer. You may leave them as they are or swirl the two together with the tip of a knife. Chill well overnight until completely set.

Serve in small wedges, quite plainly, with sliced fresh fruit or with a raspberry sauce. Decorate with chocolate leaves, if wished.

Pictured on page 81

PUDDINGS, DESSERTS AND SWEET SAUCES

LIQUEUR-GLAZED PEARS

Serves 4

Preparation time: 20 minutes + 1 hour standing + 15 minutes cooking

4 ripe pears

8 tablespoons flavoured liqueur

Almost any sweet liqueur is a success: coffee, chocolate-mint, orange, raspberry and strawberry are particularly good.

Halve each pear from top to bottom, then peel and core carefully, without cutting through the pear. Cut each half thinly from the pointed end almost to the base and press lightly to fan. Transfer to a baking sheet and pour 1 tablespoon of liqueur over each pair of halves. Leave at room temperature for about an hour.

Put the pears under a medium grill until they have lightly cooked, up to 10 minutes according to ripeness, then turn up the heat and continue cooking for 4-5 minutes until the tops have browned. Pour the remaining liqueur over the hot pears and serve at once, with ice cream or whipped cream if desired.

A Christmas Eve Meal: Braised Barbary Duck with Cranberry Red Cabbage (page 29), with Hackleback Potatoes (page 39); Liqueur-glazed Pears (page 67).

ORANGE MINCEMEAT MERINGUE TART

Preparation time: 30 minutes + 1 1/4 hours cooking — Serves 8–10

12 thin slices of seedless orange

250 g (8 oz) shortcrust pastry, thawed if frozen

1 quantity Improved Christmas Mincemeat (page 92)

3 tablespoons extra-thick marmalade

2 1/2 teaspoons orange-flower water

1/2 teaspoon ground cinnamon

a pinch of ground cloves

50 g (2 oz) ground hazelnuts

2 eggs, separated

75 g (3 oz) caster sugar

An original way to serve mincemeat. The better quality it is, the better the tart. You may use cognac or dark rum instead of orange-flower water.

Preheat the oven to Gas Mark 4/180°C/350°F. Simmer the orange slices in water until the peel is very soft, 10–20 minutes, and drain. Roll out the pastry on a lightly floured surface and use it to line a shallow 20 cm (8-inch) flan dish, preferably with a loose bottom.

Flavour the mincemeat with the marmalade and 2 teaspoons of orange-flower water. Mix in the spices, hazelnuts and egg yolks; spread the mixture on to the pastry. Arrange the cooked orange slices around the edge. Bake the tart for 35–40 minutes, until the pastry is brown and the filling set and slightly risen all over.

Remove it from the oven and reduce the temperature to Gas Mark 2/150°C/300°F. Whisk the egg whites until they form stiff peaks and then beat in the sugar tablespoon by tablespoon until the meringue is thick and glossy. Fold in the remaining 1/2 teaspoon of orange-flower water. Arrange the meringue evenly on top of the tart, beginning with the outside edge and ensuring this is absolutely sealed. This prevents the meringue from weeping. Return the tart to the oven for about 15 minutes to firm up the meringue and lightly crispen the outside. It is best served warm or cool in small slices.

Pictured on pages 44/5

POACHED CLEMENTINES WITH COGNAC RICOTTA

Serves 6

Preparation time: 15 minutes + 30–45 minutes cooking + chilling twice

6 clementines or similar fruit

600 ml (1 pint) water

250 g (8 oz) caster sugar

2–4 tablespoons cognac

125 g (4 oz) ricotta cheese

3 tablespoons flaked almonds, lightly toasted, to serve

Make these early in the festive season when clementines and other small citrus are seedless and have very thin skins. For parties it is simple to make a large amount of them, and they can be displayed in a tall pyramid, decorated with fresh citrus leaves.

Wash the fruit then prick with a sharp fork once on the top and the bottom and 4 or 5 times around the circumference. Put them into a saucepan with the water and sugar, stir over a low heat to dissolve the sugar and simmer gently, uncovered, until the skins are very soft, and a fork penetrates them like butter. This may take 30–45 minutes.

Allow the fruit to cool in the syrup and then chill for at least 4 hours, or overnight.

Mix the cognac into the ricotta. The final texture should be like whipped cream. Cut a neat cap from each clementine and stuff with the cognac ricotta. If they have collapsed, the cheese can be used to reshape them; if the inside remains intact, put the ricotta on top. Pour in a little more cognac if liked. At this stage check the consistency of the chilled syrup, which will be deliciously flavoured. If it is too sticky and thick, dilute it with water; if it is too thin and watery, boil it up again. Chill the fruit again for 1–1½ hours.

Serve each fruit with the syrup poured over and around it, perhaps with even more cognac drizzled over all and into the syrup. Scatter each serving with the flaked almonds.

Pictured on page 33

A TRADITIONAL PLUM PUDDING

Makes 2 × 1.25 kg (3 lb) puddings

Preparation time: 1 hour + 1–2 days standing + 9 hours cooking

250 g (8 oz) self-raising flour

175 g (6 oz) fresh coarse wholemeal breadcrumbs

100 g (3 1/2 oz) ground almonds

500 g (1 lb) muscovado sugar

15 g (1/2 oz) ground mixed spice

1 teaspoon ground nutmeg

1/4 teaspoon ground cloves

125 g (4 oz) unsalted butter and 300 g (10 oz) beef suet, or 425 g (14 oz) unsalted butter, chopped

1 large orange

1 small lemon

1 lime

150 ml (1/4 pint) Guinness

6 tablespoons dark rum

200 g (7 oz) cut mixed peel

375 g (12 oz) ready-to-eat prunes, chopped roughly

250 g (8 oz) sultanas or seedless raisins

250 g (8 oz) currants

250 g (8 oz) grated apple

4 eggs, beaten

1 tablespoon cognac or dark rum per person

Prunes are dried plums, and without them a Christmas pudding is not a plum pudding. This is a recipe developed over many years, based on tradition but changed slightly with the times. The great appeal is the clean, honey-like flavour given by the high citric content and spices. Because it uses some self-raising flour, it is lighter in texture than more traditional recipes. I think 1.25 kg (3 lb) is about right for 8 people, which will help you decide what size pudding bowls to use. This recipe makes 2.75 kg (6 lb).

If you give your puddings their full cooking before Christmas Day, they may be heated for serving in a microwave oven most successfully, reducing the heat and steam in the kitchen – 30 seconds per 500 g (1 lb) is usually enough but refer to your cooker's instruction book or err on the side of caution.

A silver coin for fortune, thimble for spiritual peace and a ring for marriage may be included in puddings. They are best prepared by soaking in a little household bleach, rinsing well, drying and wrapping in a strip of greaseproof paper.

Mix together the dry ingredients, rub in the butter and then stir in the suet, if using. Wash and quarter the orange, lemon and lime. Remove any pips and purée the fruits, with their skins still on, in a blender or food processor, leaving just a little coarseness. Stir the fruit into the dry ingredients with all the remaining ingredients except the eggs. Cover and leave in a cool place for a day or two, stirring from time to time.

When ready to cook, stir in the eggs. Fill the required number of pudding basins only three-quarters full, adding any coins and favours (see above). Cover the top of the mixture with a well-buttered round of greaseproof paper. Then cover the basins with foil or several layers of baking parchment or greaseproof paper, in which you have made a central pleat to allow for expansion during cooking. Tie with string, making a loop over the top for easy handling. Place a trivet in a saucepan with a tight-fitting lid. Place the pudding basin on the trivet. Carefully pour in boiling water to reach just under half-way up the basin. Cover with the lid and simmer for 2 hours per 500 g (1 lb), thus 6 hours for a 1.25 kg (3 lb) pudding; 4 hours for 1 kg (2 lb) and so on. Check the water level occasionally and top it up if necessary.

The pudding may be stored for up to 3 months in a very cool larder. If you are storing the pudding, it is best not to change the paper or foil seal after cooking as letting air into the sterile basin and pudding invites moulds.

To serve, steam the pudding for at least another hour per 500 g (1 lb); a longer time will give a darker colour. Let the pudding sit out of the water for 10 minutes or so whilst you make or complete the sauces. Then put it on to a suitable serving dish to take to the table: remove all the paper, run a knife around the inside of the bowl and turn the pudding out on to a plate with a good rim. Put a sprig of fresh holly on the top.

Heat about 1 tablespoon of cognac or dark rum per person in a small saucepan until smelling strongly of fumes. Carefully touch a lighted match to the edge of the saucepan; do not plunge your hand into the saucepan or you will be burned as the flame leaps. Pour the burning spirit gently onto and around the pudding, tipping the plate back and forth a little to ensure the flames keep going. Then carry it into the dining-room, still moving the plate a little and wearing oven gloves in case of an accident. It is good to let the flames die out themselves. If you must blow them out, do so with the utmost restraint or you will blow the fumes and flames on to the table.

The best way to get neat servings is to cut the pudding in half and then into portions. Serve with a thin custard sauce or whipped cream.

Pictured on pages 4/5

PILGRIMS' PUDDING WITH BUTTER SAUCE

Preparation time: 25 minutes + 2 hours cooking | Serves 6–8

250 g (8 oz) cranberries, blueberries or a mixture of both

75 g (3 oz) butter, chopped

50 g (2 oz) demerara sugar

2 teaspoons ground mixed spice

250 g (8 oz) self-raising flour

190 g (6 1/2 oz) treacle

5 tablespoons milk

1 teaspoon vanilla essence

For the butter sauce:

125 g (4 oz) butter

125 g (4 oz) caster or demerara sugar

142 ml (1/4 pint) carton of single cream

vanilla essence, cognac or cream sherry

I found this recipe in the United States many years ago. It's a wonderfully comforting but light pudding that has become a popular alternative to plum pudding on Christmas Day, especially with children. A marvellous way to use up cranberries and just right after a light main course at other times of the holiday season. The butter sauce is very much in the eighteenth-century tradition; these days a thin custard might be more to your taste.

Grease a 1.75-litre (3-pint) pudding basin with butter and put into the bottom a quarter of the berries and 25 g (1 oz) of the butter. Sprinkle 2 tablespoons of the sugar and 1 teaspoon of the mixed spice evenly over the top. Rub the rest of the butter into the flour. Chop the remaining berries roughly, leaving some no smaller than halves. Mix 125 g (4 oz) of these berries into the flour.

Warm the can of treacle in hot water and then measure the required amount. Mix it with the milk and add the vanilla essence. Stir the liquid into the flour just until the mixture is quite soft – do not overmix. Then transfer the mixture to the basin, and level it off. Cover with the remaining berries, sugar and spice, sprinkled evenly. Seal and cover the pudding with a cloth or foil, folding a pleat in the top to allow for expansion. Place a trivet in a saucepan with a tight-fitting lid. Place the pudding basin on the trivet. Carefully pour in boiling water to reach just under half-way up the basin. Cover with the lid and simmer for 2 hours, checking the water level occasionally and topping it up if necessary.

Combine the sauce ingredients and simmer (stirring to dissolve the sugar first) for 5 minutes, stirring occasionally until slightly thickened, although the sauce is still quite thin. Flavour to your taste with vanilla, cognac or sherry.

Pictured on pages 16/17

HOT CHESTNUT AND CHERRY SOUFFLÉS

Serves 6

Preparation time: 10 minutes + 4 hours soaking + 12–15 minutes cooking

- *411 g (14 oz) can of pitted black cherries, drained*
- *6 tablespoons dark rum, cognac or Calvados*
- *200 g (7 oz) unsweetened chestnut purée*
- *50 g (2 oz) caster sugar*
- *1 teaspoon vanilla essence*
- *250 ml (8 fl oz) double cream*
- *3 egg yolks*
- *4 egg whites*
- *1 teaspoon icing sugar*
- *1 teaspoon cocoa powder*

The simplest soufflés you will ever make: just mix and bake. The surprise base of cherries and cream means the egg can be cooked right through but the soufflés are light and moist.

Soak the cherries in the rum for at least 4 hours or overnight.

Preheat the oven to Gas Mark 6/200°C/400°F. Lightly butter 6 large ramekins about 150 ml (1/4 pint) capacity. Mix the chestnut purée, sugar and vanilla evenly with 150 ml (1/4 pint) of the cream, then whisk in the egg yolks. Put 4 cherries in the bottom of each ramekin, then evenly pour the remaining cream and the rum over them. Everything up to this stage may be prepared in advance but all must be at room temperature before continuing.

Whisk the egg whites until stiff but not dry, and fold them into the chestnut mixture. Spoon this mixture carefully into the ramekins, stand them on a baking sheet, then transfer this to the oven and cook for 12–15 minutes.

Remove the tray of ramekins and whilst still on the baking sheet lightly sieve a mixture of icing sugar and cocoa over them. Quickly put them on to folded napkins on small plates and serve at once. The remaining cherries can be passed around.

• VARIATIONS •

- There are often fresh cherries around for Christmas. If so, pit them and soak in a liqueur rather than rum – crème de cerise, crème de cacao or Tia Maria would all be good.
- If you have not served cinnamon in the other courses, add half a teaspoon to the chestnut mixture.
- The syrup from the cherries may be boiled gently until reduced to a thick syrup and served with the remaining cherries too, poured into the ramekins after the first few spoonfuls have been enjoyed; it may need a squeeze of lemon juice.

Pictured on pages 76/7

A New Year's Eve Meal: Smoked Salmon Nests with Quail Eggs (page 13); Whisky Pigeons with Barley Pilaff (page 34); Hot Chestnut and Cherry Soufflés (page 75).

EGG CUSTARD

Preparation time: 15 minutes | Serves 4–6

5 egg yolks

75 g (3 oz) caster sugar

1 teaspoon cornflour

450 ml (3/4 pint) milk

vanilla essence, cognac or liqueur

A thin custard is by far the best – and most traditional – sauce for Christmas plum puddings. Frankly there is nothing wrong with using a custard mix if that would relieve stress. Follow the packet instructions, then make it much thinner than usual by diluting with cream; flavour with vanilla and then with cognac, brandy or an orange liqueur. Allow up to 150 ml (1/4 pint) per person. Otherwise make the real thing, a velvety egg custard. Proper egg custard is best made only with yolks. Even professionals add a little cornflour to avoid being confronted with scrambled eggs, so do not hesitate to do the same.

Beat together the yolks and sugar until really pale and creamy, then stir in the cornflour. Heat the milk to boiling point and pour on to the eggs, beating all the time; this is a very important step called 'tempering', so don't be tempted to add cold milk.

Pour the custard into a saucepan and cook over a low to medium heat, stirring constantly until the mixture thickens and coats the back of a spoon. If you see any bubbles, the heat is too high. The sauce thickens as it cools to lukewarm, which is the best temperature to serve it. Keep it warm in a bowl over hot water with little or no heat underneath it. Flavour it by stirring in vanilla essence, cognac, rum or a liqueur.

RICH CUSTARD SAUCE

Preparation time: 15 minutes — Serves 4–6

284 ml (1/2 pint) carton of double cream

2 egg yolks

2 tablespoons sugar

1 tablespoon cornflour

300 ml (1/2 pint) milk, heated

vanilla essence, cognac or liqueur

Make plenty of this for it is sensational cold with fresh fruit.

Place the cream in a pan and reduce it to half its volume by boiling. Mix the yolks, sugar and cornflour together and whisk in the hot milk. Thicken the custard over a low to medium heat, stirring continuously. Add the cream and flavour the custard with vanilla essence, cognac, rum or a liqueur. Serve warm or chilled.

Pictured on pages 4/5

CUMBERLAND RUM NICKY

Preparation time: 20 minutes + 30 minutes cooking — Serves 6–8

375 g (12 oz) shortcrust pastry, thawed if frozen

250 g (8 oz) dates, stoned and roughly chopped

50 g (2 oz) glacé ginger pieces

125 g (4 oz) rum butter

A very old Cumbrian treat that uses goodies you have in the house at Christmas time. It is faster and simpler to make it as an old-fashioned plate pie; if you have more time, make a larger, lattice-top flan. It's specially good with clotted cream. Individual Nickies make an original alternative to mince pies, and were probably the origin of putting rum and brandy butter on these.

Preheat the oven to Gas Mark 6/200°C/400°F. Roll out just over half the pastry on a lightly floured surface and use it to line your chosen 20-23 cm (8- or 9-inch), deep plate or shallow pie dish. Scatter with the dates and ginger. Dot on the rum butter. Damp the pastry edges with water, top with the remaining rolled out pastry, seal the edges, slash the top and decorate. Bake for 15 minutes and then reduce the oven temperature to Gas Mark 4/180°C/350°F. Bake at the lower temperature for about 15 minutes or until the pastry is golden brown.

Pictured on page 21

DRIED FRUIT COMPÔTE WITH ROSE-WATER AND ALMONDS

Serves 6–8

Preparation time: 10 minutes + overnight standing + 10 minutes cooking

500 g (1 lb) mixed ready-to-eat dried fruits

1 cinnamon stick

1 litre (2 pints) fresh orange juice

1/2 teaspoon almond essence

1 tablespoon rose-water

To serve:

50 g (2 oz) flaked almonds, toasted lightly

3-4 tablespoons Pineau de Charentes or cognac (optional)

The simplest and most voluptuous of all desserts, combining all the best flavours brought back from the Holy Land by the Crusaders. The flavours and natural sugars combine in a rich naturally sweet syrup, a combination you can use dozens of ways. One of the best and most colourful party desserts of all and a great standby to have in the refrigerator when you have guests staying.

Combine the fruits, cinnamon stick and orange juice in a pan and bring very slowly to the boil. Simmer for 2 minutes, then remove the pan from the heat, stir in the flavourings and then transfer the mixture to a large flat-bottomed dish (approximately 1.75 litres/3 pints). Cover the dish and leave overnight at room temperature.

By now the fruit should all be plumped up and the juice should be forming a syrup. If not, add a little water and keep the compôte cool until the fruit has softened. The longer this takes the better the flavours will be. Serve small portions very cold, sprinkled with flaked almonds. A little Pineau de Charentes or cognac make specially good additions for celebrations.

Pictured on pages 44/5

• VARIATION •

Warm the fruits slowly under the grill, then turn up the grill and continue cooking until the edges have caramelised; watch carefully to ensure they don't burn. This is wonderful with ice cream.

Double Chocolate Raspberry Truffle Cake (page 66)

SHORTBREAD

Makes an 18 cm (7-inch) round

Preparation time: 10 minutes + 50 minutes cooking + cooling

125 g (4 oz) plain flour
50 g (2 oz) ground rice
1/4 teaspoon salt
125 g (4 oz) unsalted butter, chilled
50 g (2 oz) caster sugar
1 egg yolk

Shortbread is associated with New Year in Scotland, with Christmas in the rest of Britain. At this time of the year it was traditionally often made specially rich with almonds or baked with a topping of glacé fruits. Make the basic recipe, add your own fruit or try my striped version (page 94), a terrific gift idea. Either way, shortbread needs a cool kitchen, cool hands and quick work.

Preheat the oven to Gas Mark 3/160°C/325°F. Sieve the flours and salt together. Chop the butter into the flour, then rub it in. When it resembles fine breadcrumbs, stir in the sugar and bind with the egg yolk into a firm dough.

Press evenly but lightly into an 18 cm (7-inch) cake tin, lined with baking parchment. Pinch deeply all round the edge and mark into segments. Prick deeply all over, making an even pattern. Bake for up to 50 minutes in the centre of the oven or until the shortbread is an even pale golden colour. Cool before turning it out on to a wire rack to get completely cold. Sprinkle caster sugar on the top if liked.

CHRISTMAS FRUIT LOAF

Makes 2 × 500 g (1 lb) loaves or 1 stollen

Preparation time: 1 hour + proving + 35 or 55 minutes cooking

The British Yule Loaf

125 g (4 oz) sultanas

50 g (2 oz) currants

1 tablespoon dark rum

625–750 g (1 1/4–1 1/2 lb) strong white flour

15 g (1/2 oz) easy blend dried yeast

1–2 teaspoons ground mixed spice

grated zest of 1 small lemon

1 large egg, (size 1–2)

1/2 teaspoon salt

4 tablespoons caster sugar

175 g (6 oz) butter, melted and cooled, plus 40 g (1 1/2 oz)

about 300 ml (1/2 pint) milk, warmed

1 teaspoon plain flour

100 g (3 1/2 oz) chopped mixed peel

125 g (4 oz) blanched almonds, chopped

Rich yeasted loaves packed with fruit and sometimes spiced are a Christmas tradition all over Europe. In Britain they were specially popular in the North of England. Germany's best-known Christmas loaf is the stollen and the best of the many versions is said to come from Dresden. The traditional stollen shape is tapered at each end and ridged down the centre, representing the Christ Child in swaddling. Britain's version is baked in a loaf tin and always includes spice. Good long keepers, these loaves are served in very thin slices and so last well over the holiday period.

Mix the sultanas with the currants, add the rum and leave overnight.

Mix together the strong flour, yeast and spice, if using. Beat together the lemon zest, egg, salt and sugar until light, and stir into the 175 g (6 oz) melted butter. Work the butter and the milk slowly into the flour until you have a smooth, shiny dough. You may have to add extra flour to make it manageable. Knead the dough for 5 minutes, then leave it to double in size in a warm place, covered with a damp tea towel. This too may be left overnight, in which case the position should be cool, even a refrigerator; if so, return the dough to room temperature before continuing.

Preheat the oven to Gas Mark 6/200°C/400°F. Divide the dough into 2 pieces. Toss the sultanas and currants in the teaspoon of plain flour. Mix them with the peel and the almonds and scatter these between the pieces of dough on a floured surface. Then knead gently to distribute them.

Put the dough into 2 lightly greased 500 g (1 lb) loaf tins, cover with a damp tea towel and leave to rise. Bake the loaves for about 35 minutes, covering loosely with foil if they are browning too quickly.

Test that the loaves are cooked through using a

skewer or by turning them and tapping firmly; if they sound hollow, they are cooked. Remove them from the oven and brush with the remaining 40 g (1½ oz) melted butter, whilst warm. Loosen the sides of the loaves and turn them out on to a wire rack. If they are kept well wrapped in an airtight container they can last for over a month. Serve very thinly sliced, with or without butter.

• VARIATION •

The Stollen
1 quantity British Yule Loaf dough
250 g (8 oz) marzipan (optional)
40 g (1½ oz) butter, melted, to glaze
caster sugar and icing sugar, for dusting

Preheat the oven to Gas Mark 6/200°C/400°F. Roll out the dough into an oval about 2.5 cm (1 inch) thick. Put this on to a large, greased baking sheet. Make an indentation down the centre with the edge of your hand and add the marzipan, if using, forming it into a roll the same length as the oval and flattening it slightly. Fold the right-hand third of the dough over the rest. Fold the left-hand side over that; it will not go all the way to the right-hand side. Press down firmly. Use the edges of both hands to press up a round ridge from top to bottom, that tapers and thins the same way the dough does. Press hard either side of this to exaggerate the difference. Fold under the top and bottom to make nice points. Paint with a little of the melted butter, cover with a damp tea towel and allow to double in size.

Bake the stollen for about 55 minutes to 1 hour. It should not be too coloured, so cover it loosely with foil after the first 15 minutes of cooking. Test that the stollen is cooked through using a skewer or by turning it and tapping it firmly; if it sounds hollow, it is cooked. Remove it from the oven and brush it with the remaining melted butter, dust with caster sugar and then icing sugar whilst warm. Transfer it to a wire rack and allow to cool.

If it is kept well wrapped in an airtight container, the stollen can last for over 1 month. Serve it very thinly sliced, with or without butter.

A Christmas Tea Party: Walnut Layer Cake (page 86); Kendal Gingerbread (page 87); Chocolate Ginger Shortbread (page 94).

WALNUT LAYER CAKE

Makes 2 × 20 cm (8-inch) cakes

Preparation time: 25 minutes + 20–25 minutes cooking + cooling

125 g (4 oz) butter

250 g (8 oz) caster sugar

4 eggs, beaten

15 g (1/2 oz) baking powder

300 g (10 oz) plain flour

150 ml (1/4 pint) milk

1/2 teaspoon vanilla essence

50 g (2 oz) chopped walnuts

For the filling:

1 scant tablespoon ginger ale

1/2 teaspoon vanilla essence

25 g (1 oz) walnuts, chopped very finely

4 tablespoons apricot jam

For the icing:

1 tablespoon ginger ale

175 g (6 oz) icing sugar, sifted

25 g (1 oz) walnut halves, toasted

A lovely old-fashioned cake I found amongst the handwritten recipes of a retired cookery teacher. Walnut cakes are a terrifically popular British tradition. This one does not include the usual coffee flavouring, but uses ginger ale in the filling and icing – much nicer I think.

Grease and bottom-line 2 × 20 cm (8-inch) cake tins. Preheat the oven to Gas Mark 4/180°C/350°F. Cream the butter and sugar together thoroughly and then add the eggs one by one, beating well between additions. Sift the baking powder and flour together. Fold into the mixture alternately with the milk and vanilla. Fold in the walnuts. Divide the mixture between the 2 prepared tins and bake for 20–25 minutes until the cakes have started to shrink from the sides and spring back when touched. Leave them in the tins for 5 minutes, then turn out on to a wire rack to cool completely.

Mix together the filling ingredients and use to join the 2 halves. Stir the ginger ale into the icing sugar and spread over the top section. Decorate with walnut halves.

KENDAL GINGERBREAD

Preparation time: 20 minutes + 10–15 minutes cooking Makes 20 biscuits

75 g (3 oz) plain flour

75 g (3 oz) ground rice

1 heaped teaspoon ground ginger

1/4 teaspoon ground allspice

1/4 teaspoon baking powder

125 g (4 oz) butter, chopped

50 g (2 oz) demerara or muscovado sugar

25 g (1 oz) candied peel, chopped finely

a little milk or egg

1 tablespoon caster sugar

Cumbria has loved ginger in cooking ever since her ports became the principal landing place for imports from Jamaica and the New World. Traditional gingerbread from a secret recipe is still made and sold from a cottage in Grasmere, but this seems almost the same. A wonderful, old-fashioned flavour, ideal for gifts.

Preheat the oven to Gas Mark 4/180°C/350°F. Mix the flour, ground rice, spices and baking powder together. Rub in the butter until the mixture resembles fine breadcrumbs, then stir in the demerara or muscovado sugar and peel. Mix together with your hands, pressing lightly to form a ball. Knead very lightly until smooth. Roll out on a lightly floured surface to no more than 5 mm (1/4 inch) thick and cut into shapes. Christmas shapes, such as stars or trees, would be good, using biscuit cutters or a template. Transfer the biscuits to one or more baking sheets, then brush them with a little milk or egg and sprinkle with caster sugar. Bake for 10–15 minutes. Allow to cool for a few minutes on a wire rack.

GRAND CHRISTMAS CAKE

Makes a 25 cm (10-inch) cake

Preparation time: 15 minutes + 3½–4 hours cooking + 2 weeks 'feeding'

375 g (12 oz) unsalted butter

250 g (8 oz) demerara or soft brown sugar

4 eggs

375 g (12 oz) plain flour

½ teaspoon ground nutmeg

½ teaspoon ground mace

½ teaspoon ground cloves

250 g (8 oz) seedless raisins

250 g (8 oz) sultanas

200 g (7 oz) mixed peel

200 g (7 oz) glacé cherry pieces

125 g (4 oz) ground almonds

grated zest of 2 sweet oranges and 1 lemon

5 tablespoons orange liqueur

5 tablespoons cognac or brandy, plus extra for 'feeding'

A new variation on my favourite traditional cake, based on a Victorian original from a royal chef. Using only sultanas and seedless raisins gives a light colour but a richer, more mellow flavour than you get with currants. This is a cake guaranteed never to be heavy or sickly.

Line a deep 25 cm (10-inch) cake tin with several layers of greased greaseproof paper or greased baking parchment. Preheat the oven to Gas Mark 1/140°C/275°F.

Cream the butter thoroughly, then beat in the sugar, followed by the eggs. Sieve the flour and spices and fold into the mixture. Add the other ingredients, stirring evenly. The mixture should have a stiff dropping consistency; if not stir in a little extra cognac. Spoon into the prepared tin and bake for 3½ to 4 hours, until a skewer inserted into the centre will come out clean. Cover the top with greaseproof paper during the latter stages of cooking if it is getting too brown.

Allow to cool completely in the tin, then take it out, discard the paper, clean the tin and reline. Put the cake back in and skewer the cake from top to bottom all over, then 'feed' it with 5 tablespoons of alcohol, using the back of the spoon to encourage absorption. Wrap the cake in greaseproof paper and then in foil. Allow to mature in a cool dark place for 2 weeks, feeding once or twice more.

Cover with almond paste, flavoured with orange-flower water, and/or icing in your favourite way. You need about 4.5 kg (2½ lb) of each. It is simpler and more fun to decorate with Christmas tree baubles, ribbons and fancy cut-outs.

Grand Christmas Cake

PRESERVED GINGER CAKE

Makes a 20 cm (8-inch) square cake

Preparation time: 25 minutes + 40–50 minutes cooking + cooling

2 tablespoons golden syrup

4 tablespoons preserved ginger syrup

3 eggs

175 g (6 oz) butter, softened

175 g (6 oz) caster sugar

250 g (8 oz) self-raising flour

2 teaspoons ground ginger

25 g (1 oz) ground almonds

50 g (2 oz) preserved stem ginger, chopped

extra preserved ginger syrup

1 tablespoon ginger wine or sweet sherry

preserved or crystallised ginger, to decorate

A marvellous alternative to fruit cakes that still has a festive flavour. A perfect New Year's Eve cake, using up the ginger in syrup which is always left over after Christmas. It's bound to become a tradition in your house, too.

Preheat the oven to Gas Mark 4/180°C/350°F. Lightly grease and line a 20 cm (8-inch) square cake tin. Warm the syrups in a small pan and beat into the eggs. Cream the butter and sugar together thoroughly and gradually beat in the syrup mixture. Sift the flour and ginger together and fold in, half at a time. Then fold in the almonds. Add the chopped ginger, being careful not to overmix. Spoon the mixture gently into the cake tin, level off the top with the back of a spoon and bake in the oven for 45–50 minutes.

Test with a skewer to ensure it is cooked through. Cool for 10 minutes before turning out on to a wire rack. Whilst still slightly warm, puncture the cake all over with a skewer and paint on a few teaspoonfuls of ginger syrup mixed with ginger wine or sherry. This can be repeated. Decorate with thinly sliced or chopped preserved ginger or some crystallised ginger.

LUXURIOUS GLAZED CHRISTMAS CAKE

Makes a 22 cm (8½-inch) square or a 23 cm (9-inch) round cake

Preparation time: 50 minutes + 2 hours cooking

250 g (8 oz) ready-to-eat prunes

100 g (3½ oz) ready-to-eat dried peaches

100 g (3½ oz) ready-to-eat dried apricots

200 g (7 oz) sultanas

250 g (8 oz) seedless raisins

100 g (3½ oz) currants

100 g (3½ oz) chopped dates

250 ml (8 fl oz) oloroso or cream sherry

2 heaped tablespoons morello cherry jam

4 tablespoons brandy

125 g (4 oz) unsalted butter, softened

125 g (4 oz) muscovado sugar

3 eggs

1 teaspoon ground cinnamon

1 teaspoon ground nutmeg

½ teaspoon ground cloves

12 cardamom pods

175 g (6 oz) plain flour

125 g (4 oz) self-raising flour

2 tablespoons cocoa powder

200 g (7 oz) chopped mixed peel

200 g (7 oz) glacé cherry pieces

A simple cake to make, this combines the best of a variety of un-iced Christmas cakes I have found in my travels. From Australia comes the idea of including prunes, dried peaches and apricots. Sri Lanka makes a spiced Christmas cake with cardamom, cinnamon and cloves. In the United States cocoa powder, pecan nuts and cherries are the secret. By using ready-to-eat dried fruits there is no need to soak them in advance and there is no need to line the tin or heat the oven in advance – you do this after making the mixture. This recipe gives a rich moist cake that is cooked but deliciously sticky in the middle. You could bake it for a further 1½–2 hours when it will still be moist but have a firmer texture and much darker colour. It may be eaten the next day but definitely keeps and improves for up to 3 months if kept tightly wrapped in an airtight cake tin.

Coarsely slice the prunes, peaches and apricots then put them into a large bowl with the sultanas, raisins, currants and dates. Pour on the sherry, mix well and leave to stand.

Mix the morello cherry jam with the brandy until smooth. Cream the butter and sugar together, then quickly add the eggs one by one – do not beat more than absolutely necessary to mix together. Stir in the cherry/brandy mixture and the ground spices.

Split the cardamom pods and grind the seeds using a pestle and mortar. Add to the mixture. Combine the flours and cocoa powder. Sieve and fold into the mixture in 3 lots. Drain the soaking fruit, reserving the liquid. Mix in the fruit, adding the peel, cherry pieces, ginger and nuts.

Prepare your 22 cm (8½-inch) square or a 23 cm (9-inch) round cake tin with 3 layers of baking parchment or lightly greased greaseproof paper. Then turn on the oven to Gas Mark 3/160°C/325°F whilst you clear up.

Spoon the mixture into the tin and bake the

100 g (3½ oz) glacé ginger pieces

50 g (2 oz) chopped hazelnuts, roasted

100 g (3½ oz) pecan nuts, chopped roughly

cake in the centre of the oven for 2 hours, perhaps covering the top with greaseproof paper after the first hour.

When the cake is cooked, sprinkle the reserved liquid from soaking the fruit over the top and let it cool completely in the tin.

ORIGINAL MINCE PIES

Makes about 24 small pies or a 20 cm (8-inch) pie

Preparation time: 20 minutes + 35–40 minutes cooking

BASIC 'IMPROVED' CHRISTMAS MINCEMEAT

411 g (14 oz) jar of mincemeat

2 tablespoons extra-thick marmalade

½ teaspoon ground cinnamon

¼ teaspoon ground cardamom

50 g (2 oz) ground almonds, hazelnuts or walnuts

Options:

2 teaspoons or more of any of the following:
orange-flower water;
half orange-flower and half rose-water;
vanilla or almond essence;
grated orange zest;
grated lime zest;
grated chocolate.

2 tablespoons or more of any of the following:
dark rum;
cognac;
orange liqueur;
coffee liqueur.

Christmas mincemeats containing beef suet or vegetarian suet are excellent these days, and many people use them instead of making their own. I like to go half-way: buy mincemeat and then make it my own. I use Mrs Beeton's basic ploy and then add extra twists, all of which make it rather less sweet. A simple but effective option is to use the mincemeat as you find it but to flavour the butter for the pastry with grated orange zest or ground cardamom.

Put the basic 'improved' mincemeat ingredients in a large mixing bowl and mix your chosen flavourings in thoroughly. Here are some of my particular favourites:

- ground almonds and grated orange zest;
- ground almonds, dark rum and fresh pineapple;
- ground walnuts, cognac and fresh apple.

To make small pies: preheat the oven to Gas Mark 7/220°C/425°F. Roll out the larger quantity of shortcrust pastry, cut into shapes and use to line greased mince pie tins. Add a heaped teaspoon of filling, cover the pies with their lids and glaze with beaten egg or milk. Bake for 20 minutes, then reduce the temperature to Gas Mark 4/180°C/350°F and continue cooking for 15–20 minutes.

A far easier way, to my mind, is to make large pies, with bases of shortcrust pastry and puff pastry tops. These amounts will nicely fill an 18 or 20 cm (7- or 8-inch) shallow pie dish. Preheat the

Toffee-apple and Walnut Pie (page 63)

And/or:

125 g (4 oz) ready-to-eat dried apricots or prunes, sliced;

175 g (6 oz) fresh pineapple, chopped;

175 g (6 oz) apple, chopped or grated;

175 g (6 oz) orange, chopped;

174 g (6 oz) raspberries or blueberries.

For the pastry:

250 g (8 oz) shortcrust pastry, plus 250 g (8 oz) puff pastry, or 500 g (1 lb) shortcrust pastry

a little beaten egg or milk

oven to Gas Mark 7/220°C/425°F. Bake for 20 minutes and then reduce the heat to Gas Mark 4/180°C/350°F and cook for a further 15–20 minutes.

CHOCOLATE GINGER SHORTBREAD

Makes 16 pieces

Preparation time: 35 minutes + 25–30 minutes cooking + cooling

ingredients for 2 quantities shortbread mixture (page 82)

50 g (2 oz) glacé ginger pieces

1 tablespoon cocoa powder

Preheat the oven to Gas Mark 3/160°C/325°F. Make 1 shortbread mixture, adding the ginger pieces with the sugar. Make the second mixture and add the cocoa powder with the dry ingredients. Roll out each of the doughs to a rectangle 30 × 40 cm (12 × 16 inches) on a lightly floured surface. Put the ginger shortbread on top of the chocolate. Cut in half widthways and put one half on the other, again with the ginger layer on top. Trim the edges. Transfer to a baking sheet and cut in half lengthways again to make 2 neat strips of about 30 × 10 cm (12 × 4 inches). Separate the 2 pieces, then mark each into 8 bars, using the back of a knife. Prick each bar deeply. Bake for 25–30 minutes. Cool before turning it out on to a wire rack to get completely cold.

For a different effect, roll each of the final oblongs from its longer side and cut through with a sharp knife to make 8 shortbread swirls. These will take rather less time to cook, 20–30 minutes.

INDEX TO RECIPES

Cover design: Barry Lowenhoff
Text design: Ken Vail Graphic Design
Photography: Tim Imrie
Stylist: Anna Tait
Food preparation for photography: Louise Pickford
Illustration: John Woodcock
Typesetting: Designer Types